Find the Love of Your Life

Also by Julia Cole and published by Help Yourself

Make Love Work for You:
An Essential Guide for Career Couples

Find the Love
of Your Life

Julia Cole

Hodder & Stoughton
LONDON SYDNEY AUCKLAND

British Library Cataloguing in Publication Data
A record for this book is available from the British Library

ISBN 0 340 74596 7

Typeset by Avon Dataset Ltd, Bidford-on-Avon, Warks

Printed and bound in Great Britain by
The Guernsey Press Co. Ltd, Channel Isles

Hodder & Stoughton
A Division of Hodder Headline Ltd
338 Euston Road
London NW1 3BH

For Peter, the love of my life

Contents

Acknowledgments

I wish to express my thanks to all those who helped to make this book possible: to Judith Longman of Hodder & Stoughton for her invitation to write this book and her hard work in bringing it to fruition; to Jo Frank, my agent, for her expert advice and help in all my writing endeavours; and to Adam and Hannah, with thanks for all their patience.

Acknowledgments

Introduction

Are you searching for the perfect partner? The love of your life? Have you often wondered why a first date went wrong, or how to make a good date even better? Do you want to know how to judge if your new partner is really right for you, or whether you should sleep with someone on the first date or the hundredth? If so, this is the book for you.

This book is about how to search for the partner who will suit you and what to do when you find them. Despite the predictions about marriage declining in the future and a rising divorce rate, one thing is sure – people still want to give and receive love, and they are still looking for the one relationship that will make them feel secure, happy and satisfied. It is tempting to imagine that once we reach puberty, the skills we need to handle new relationships magically pop into our heads, allowing us to manage the ups and downs of dating and relating. The truth is that most of us muddle through, often making mistakes, sometimes learning from them, but more often repeating them again with our next boyfriend or girlfriend. And with the increased prevalence of second marriages, or committed relationships, after a previous relationship breakdown, the problems of finding and maintaining a new relationship can be legion.

It is true that couples have been finding each other, falling in love, falling out of love and creating families or building new relationships since time immemorial. There is nothing new about love. But we do face special couple concerns in the twenty-first century. Nowadays, both men and women are likely to work. We live in a communications age, where everything is done at breakneck speed. The luxury of taking time to get to know another person in a relaxed way is something that many of us feel has slipped away. The aim of this book is to help you get back in touch with some important ways of thinking about new relationships, to give you the confidence you need to find new people to meet and then to get a new relationship off to the best possible start.

Find the Love of Your Life begins by explaining the nature of modern relationships and explains some of the changes that have assailed couples in recent years. Chapter One looks at the influences on people seeking to find a partner – from personal and family influences to celebrity romances and break-ups. Chapter Two moves on to ask what you want from a relationship, and how this has influenced your choice of partner. This chapter will help you to reflect on your character and personality, what kind of partner you have previously chosen and what would be good for you. Your self-perception is also discussed, followed by ideas for tackling negative self-perception. Chapter Three looks in detail at what you are carrying in your personal 'back pack' and whether this weighs you down or helps you climb the mountain to find love. Practical suggestions for common relationship problems are also addressed. Chapter Four offers a breakdown of the usual ways in which people find partners, and the various merits of approaching these. Chapter Five takes an in-depth look at first date behaviour, examines some of the problems and helps you to make good use of the things that work. This chapter contains a safe dating practice checklist and how to read the unspoken signs about your potential partner's character. Chapter Six looks at the difficult issue of sexual etiquette in new relationships. This chapter includes how to assess when the relationship is ready for sex and information on safe sex practices, as well as the impact on others when you decide to create an intimate relationship, with special reference to the children of any previous relationship. Chapter Seven will help you to decide if this is the right relationship for you and offers ways of thinking about what you want from the future of a new relationship. Chapter Eight includes some typical questions about dating and finding new love, together with answers that will enable you to solve particular difficulties.

My hope is that this book will provide an invaluable guide as you search for a loving partner, establish a new relationship and then decide what you want in the future of the partnership. Start reading now – the love of your life could be just around the corner!

1

Finding and Sustaining New Relationships

This book is about finding the love of your life. The 'your' part is the most important part of the title of this book. If we were all emotional robots, there would be no problem in finding a partner. We could feed our programs into a 'love computer', it would dial up a suitable mate and soon we would have lots of little robots running around! Fortunately, this sci-fi vision is unlikely ever to see the light of day. Humans are complex and subtle. We need to make relationships with people who make us happy, support us in tough times and, most of all, suit our unique personality and character. Human beings also change as they mature and age. In a committed relationship, our choice of partner needs to satisfy us over a long period of time, so to steal an RSPCA slogan, 'A partner should be for life (or at least a long time), not just for Christmas'!

Satisfying relationships allow us to enjoy life to the full. Un-happy relationships drain us, making life seem grey and stressful. The key to creating a happy relationship lies in choosing the right person. Like laying the foundations of a house, the way in which you choose a partner, and understanding why you make the choices you do, can make or break a relationship. And this relationship will be unique. You are the person who will make the ultimate choice. But many people enter into relationships that are completely unsuitable for them. Sometimes their choice is impulsive – perhaps going out with someone they know in their heart is not really right for them, but finding they cannot say no. Others link up with a partner not for love, but because they think they might be 'left on the shelf'. Some couples even choose each other out of fear – fear of the fall-out from families and friends if they do not choose the person their relatives approve of, or if they break up with someone that their friends think is just right for them. Making the right choice can be difficult, but this book will guide you through all you need to know about finding and nurturing a new relationship that is just right for you.

Love in the New Millennium

About 25 per cent of men and women over 16 in the UK are currently single, and about 30 per cent of all men and women in the UK have never been married. At least some of these are cohabiting – about 13 per cent – and this number is set to rise dramatically in the next decade. The number of single-person households has risen from 17 per cent in 1971 to 29 per cent in 1998. These figures tell us that, as we go into a new millennium, we are living in a demographic revolution.

At the beginning of the twentieth century, most adults were married. Marriage was expected by society and the church, and seen as the *only* choice if you wanted to be with a partner. It is true that some bohemian individuals chose to live together without being married, but these people often existed in an inner circle connected to the arts. Poorer and disadvantaged groups of people may also not have married, but this was generally regarded as outside the norm and brought with it some severe sanctions – the illegitimacy of children born to such a couple, for instance. They risked social disgrace and were looked down upon by the 'respectable' middle classes. Same sex cohabiting relationships were a source of scandal and often led to social ruin for those who attempted them – witness what happened to the author and playwright Oscar Wilde who, although married with a wife and two children, was vilified and imprisoned for his homosexual relationships. As the twentieth century progressed, social change advanced in leaps and bounds. Two world wars, equality for women, better contraception and gradually improving racial equality caused people to look at social institutions such as marriage, that they had once revered, with new eyes. The liberalism of the 1960s initiated new ways of being in a couple, and this has led many people to question old ideas about how a couple should live in the twenty-first century. Cohabitation, gay and lesbian partnerships, married couples without children, unmarried couples with children – we accept all of these as part and parcel of modern life. Many of the restrictive barriers that our parents and grandparents took for granted have come tumbling down. Of course, not all of the population think this is good, but the notion that people can be free to explore and find the partnership that is right for them, rather than having to fit into an uncomfortable social mould, seems to be fast gaining ground. Just as we have moved away from starched collars and corsets to stretch lycra and T-shirts, so we have relaxed what we expect of each other in terms of relationships.

But despite all this change, one crucial element remains. You can guess what this is from a casual glance at TV, listening to chart music or from a visit to the cinema. People still want to feel loved and to give love to one another. They mostly want their relationship to be special, usually exclusive, and to be marked by faithfulness. We are still seeking 'the one' in exactly the same way as our ancestors did. Interestingly, although just about every love song ever written eulogises this state of 'being in love', it has become common to see long-term relationships as boring, and possibly to be avoided! There is a common assumption that every long-term relationship loses the shine of the new relationship, and that this signs the death warrant to romance. We are all 'love junkies' now. Advertising and popular culture tells us that if our relationship no longer induces that 'butterflies in the stomach' feeling then we should dump it and move on to the next person. The problem with this approach is that we may never learn how to make a judgement about who is right for us; we are paying so much attention to the emotional high that new love induces that our critical faculties become clouded. Added to this is the pressure of trying to come first in a kind of 'Sex Olympics'! Of course, our parents and grandparents had sex but it never received the kind of concentrated attention that this generation has paid to it. Depending on your viewpoint, this is the sign of a society becoming more comfortable with sexual matters or one that is unhealthily obsessed with sex. My experience of counselling couples with sexual concerns is that, despite all the sexual hype surrounding us, many people find it very difficult to develop a sexual communication that suits them and that helps them to express themselves as they want to. It is as if we have accepted all the talk about sex as being like a 'one size fits all' sweatshirt, when in reality sexual relationships have to be tailored to fit each new partnership.

It also seems that individuals are finding it harder to make new relationships. This is probably due to a number of changes in society, especially changes in women's roles. Women have become more choosy about who they make relationships with. The majority of 'live alone' homes are occupied by women. The anxiety that women of previous generations endured, of being without financial security if they were not with a man, has all but vanished. Lone women are much more able to maintain themselves, and this has resulted in fewer women marrying only in order to avoid money worries. Women are also less likely than men to put up with an unhappy marriage. Over 70 per cent of all divorces are initiated by women. Despite this, the number of second and subsequent marriages is escalating, so many women are far from turned off the idea of marriage by divorce. These changes, and others, have left men also asking what they want from relationships. Some men feel threatened by the idea of powerful women making their own decisions. Some aspects of the 'lad culture' that has grown up in the last few years seem to bear witness to this. These men want to club together under the banner of sport or drinking to shut out the truth – that independent, strong women are here to stay. Other men are happy to embrace the changes, but are not really sure what the women they meet expect of them. Do women want an all-action hero or a sensitive gentleman? To be fair, women seem a bit confused about this themselves! Indeed, they may feed their prospective partner several mixed messages – I want you to be James Bond today and Mr Darcy tomorrow!

All of these changes have meant that many men and women are desperate to choose the right partner, but simply feel baffled by all the different influences on them as they try to make that choice. Should they choose someone who is a brilliant lover? Someone who is secure in their work? Someone who makes them laugh? Or someone who they may only stay with for a few months before moving on? These questions represent only a fraction of the hundreds that most people ask themselves when they begin dating and mating. This book will help you to unravel what kind of relationship you really want and then give you ideas on how to make it happen.

Why love is still on-line

It is an interesting question as to why we still seek couple relationships. Given that we can now have relationships to which we are not necessarily tied for life, and that women have the potential to give birth through IVF, what still pulls us into a committed partnership? Here are some reasons why couple relationships are still popular.

Biology
It is likely that at least part of our desire to be in a partnership is genetic. Our forebears formed couple relationships because of the joint benefits. The female got cared for during her pregnancy and child-rearing time – a time of vulnerability to attack from predators – and the male had at least some certainty that the offspring were his.

Cultural
As biology dictated some of our basic behaviour, so culture and tradition added to this imperative. It became expected that people would bond in couples to raise a family. In some societies, this is

not exactly the same – for instance, some cultures still feel it is OK to have more than one wife. But for the most part, couple relationships are the norm all over the world.

Emotional

The desire to feel special to just one person is understood by most people. This may have its roots in our early relationship to our mother. In other words, we may seek to replicate this deep relationship to the first person to care for us (although this does not necessarily have to be our biological mother – foster and adoptive parents can often give this intense kind of love). This does not mean that we want to be 'mothered', but that we may seek that extremely close connection that we once experienced. It is also true that as a couple, people often feel they can take on the world in a way that they might not feel as confident about if they were on their own. They know they have someone to rejoice, and to share problems, with. This can offer emotional security in a world that is becoming increasingly stressful.

Health

Statistics demonstrate that single people (particularly men) are more likely to suffer from a range of illnesses than those in couple relationships. Depression, heart disease, some cancers and drug and alcohol addictions have all been shown to be more prevalent in single people. These findings are even more strongly associated with separated and divorced people. This group is even more likely to suffer ill health than those who lose a partner through bereavement.

Shared parenting

The proportion of births outside marriage has increased dramatically. A third of all births are now to unmarried mothers – more than four times the proportion of the early 1970s. Single parenting (usually by lone mothers) has also increased in recent years. Although many births are now to unmarried mothers, most are registered by both partners. The notion that couples should care for children as a shared enterprise has not lost its popularity, and is still one of the benefits of a couple relationship – married or unmarried. There is not much doubt that raising a child alone can be difficult and that sharing the load in some way is usually a better option than struggling on single-handed. This is not to suggest that many lone parents do not make an excellent job of nurturing their children, but much research over the last twenty years has found that even the best organised lone parent often feels that they would like to share some of the burdens of parenting.

How did you learn about relationships?

There are clearly benefits in being part of a couple, but many people do live single lives and are very happy with this arrangement. For some, being alone is an active choice – they have decided not to find a permanent partner. For others, being single was not intended and is perhaps due to a bereavement or break-up with a partner. Many people regard their single status as an interim arrangement; a stage before finding a partner. Whatever your experience, if you are hoping to find a partner one day it is important to try and understand how you think about relationships. If you can do this well before you meet a prospective partner you will understand where you are coming from. This is useful information. For instance, if your only experience of relationships in the past has been that you are likely to be let down, then you may either set yourself up to fail, or have very low expectations of your new friend.

Here are some pertinent questions to ask yourself about what you know about relationships, and how you have absorbed this over the years. You could find it useful to make some notes about each question before reading the section beneath it. In this way, you can compare your own responses to the help given under each question.

What did I learn about relationships from my parents' marriage/relationship?

The first place we learn about relationships is in the family we are born into (or raised by). When it comes to relating to others, children absorb information like sponges as they grow up. They watch their parents and other members of the family talking to each other and living together. This begins at a very early age – from babyhood onwards. Children are often very aware of emotional atmosphere in a family, even when their parents think they are hiding some aspect of their partnership. Think about whether your home life was warm or cool, whether affection was shown openly, whether your parents praised or criticised each other. You should also consider whether or not they seemed to share domestic tasks, and how this was decided, and how they approached work concerns. Parents who can communicate successfully, and talk through their difficulties to find a resolution, give a positive example of how to make a relationship work. Those couples who play power games with each other, or have rigid ideas of how a partnership should be organised, can leave a legacy that their children may find very hard to counteract once they make their own relationships. If your parents had affairs or breached trust in some other way, you may also have formed your own ideas about whether you should trust others, and to what extent. If you have come from foster care or a children's home, you may lack these images, or have others which feel somehow alien to you. All of these observations of your parents' relationship, conscious or unconscious, will be crowding at the back of your mind when you set eyes on an attractive stranger. Whether you like it or not, they will influence your choice and then how the relationship develops.

CASE STUDY

Darren and Judy, both 22, met in a nightclub in their home town. They had known each other at school, but taken very little notice of each other at that time. In fact, when Darren first approached Judy, he did not recognise her as the girl he had known at school. But he soon realised that she was going to be more than just another ex-schoolfriend. Judy also saw Darren as important. She felt they just clicked with one another very quickly. They began to see each other several times a week. After a number of months, Judy suggested to Darren that they should move in together, and it was at this point that the trouble started. Judy found it very difficult to talk to Darren about almost anything. She often took action that Darren found puzzling. On one occasion she ordered a new bed without even asking him if he thought this was necessary. Darren and Judy began to fight over this issue, and after a particularly exhausting row, with Judy in tears, Darren asked if her parents also argued in the same way. Judy admitted that they often fought over similar problems. Judy's mum took all the decisions in the family, rarely asking her father for his opinion. Although this did cause upsets, her father seemed to accept the situation. Judy had always sworn that she would never do the same thing, seeing her mother as a 'control freak', and was horrified at the realisation that she was duplicating this behaviour. Darren agreed to try to help Judy to develop new ways of taking joint decisions, and their relationship became less volatile.

How have my friends' and other relatives' relationships affected me?

As you have grown up, you will have watched your friends, brothers, sisters and other relatives, entering into relationships. You may have approved of their choices, or decided they had definitely made the wrong choice. Watching them talk to (or argue with!) one another will have been, or may still be, an influence on you. If a sibling's relationship has broken down you may find this has jaundiced your attitude to partnerships, or made you want to find a secure partnership for yourself. You could also find that you admire certain aspects of a friend's relationship, actively seeking to have these in your own partnership. You may develop feelings of jealousy about a friend's relationship, especially if your own partnership is not going very well, or a desire to protect a relative if their relationship is in trouble. All of these experiences will add to your own blueprint of what you look for in a new relationship.

CASE STUDY

Rob and Sandy began going out after Rob met Sandy at a conference connected to his work as a manager in a car plant. They felt an immediate attraction to one another and arranged to meet the following weekend. They enjoyed going out and were soon regarded as a couple by most of their friends. After some months, Rob asked Sandy to meet his family at a barbecue held at his elder brother's home. As soon as they arrived at Alan's, Sandy sensed there was a problem. Rob seemed prickly and withdrawn, spending most of his time nursing a can of beer in the corner of the garden. Sandy was treated courteously by Rob's family, but felt as if she and Rob were very much outsiders. On the car journey home, Sandy asked Rob what had happened. Rob explained that Fran, his sister-in-law, was Alan's second wife. Alan had had an affair with Fran years before, leaving his first wife and baby son in order to live with Fran. Rob had told Alan he thought he was behaving appallingly, and hardly spoke to him for years. Sandy asked Rob how this had affected his attitude to relationships. Rob explained that he had found it hard to make close relationships for quite some time – in fact, Sandy was the first for three years – partly because he wondered if it was possible to really know someone. He had believed that he knew Alan well, but felt this notion had been destroyed when Alan left his first wife. Rob's attitude to relationships had been affected by a betrayal of his trust in Alan, followed by feelings of doubt that any partnership could ever really be rock solid.

Where else have I learnt about relationships?

Pick up any magazine or turn on the TV and you will find that there are pages of relationship advice jumping out at you. Chat shows where audience members bare their souls, magazine stories about couples who have beaten overwhelming odds, or kiss-and-tell articles in newspapers, all give us messages about how relationships should be conducted. The problem with many of these messages is that they are contradictory. Sometimes we learn that it is always wrong to have an affair, while at other times we are told it can ginger up a marriage. Women are sometimes portrayed as victims, at other times as scheming or totally in control. It is no wonder that many people embarking on new relationships feel confused about how to proceed. If you read media articles or watch TV, ask yourself what you feel you have learnt from these. Then try to decide if you agree with their messages, or if the attitudes you have picked up help or hinder your approach to forming relationships. You may have been lucky enough to have received good relationship education at school. (I would like to emphasise 'relationship' here – many of us received biology lessons about reproduction, but precious little information about how the theory fits into real human relations.) If you had relationship education, or biology lessons, think through what you learnt from it. Did it improve your confidence in relationships, or give you pause for thought? What key messages did you take away from it? For example, you may have been told that sex is dangerous because of sexually transmitted diseases or that being married is the only 'right' relationship.

CASE STUDY

Diana was a divorcee who longed for a new relationship, but as it was fifteen years since she had been on the dating scene she lacked self-confidence. She found that she bought magazines, searching for true life stories that were similar to hers, in order to boost her confidence. Although Diana did occasionally find stories that described successful love the second time around, she also found items that described the pitfalls of starting a new relationship after divorcing. Diana felt confused until she spotted an advert for a new kind of dating agency especially aimed at people like herself who were returning to dating after some years. She signed up, and soon began to meet men who had the potential to be future boyfriends. Diana felt that the articles in the magazines had prompted her to think about going out with men again, but she had some reservations about the advice they gave as not all of it accorded with her own experience.

Have I been influenced by people in the public eye?

Fifty years ago this question might have elicited the response, 'Yes, the royal family.' At this time, many people saw the King, Queen and two little princesses, Elizabeth and Margaret, as the epitome of family life. Since then, a galaxy of film stars, musicians, TV celebrities and many others, seemingly famous for being famous, have influenced how we think about relationships. Their marriages, divorces, make-ups and break-ups are daily fodder for the tabloid newspapers and are bound to influence us to some degree, even if we would like to think that we are immune to their behaviour. For instance, we may applaud a famous star for divorcing their violent partner, or condemn a member of a boy band who has an affair with a TV presenter. It is possible that seeing the particular lifestyle of famous people has made you feel that you want the same kind of lifestyle. This could prevent you from settling with any relationship that does not match the same standards. Some of this may be unconscious – you may not realise that reading about or watching your favoured star has touched you at all. Or you may consciously imitate their behaviour. Whatever the case, now is the time to ask yourself if this influence is helpful, giving you a positive role model, or a negative one, and preventing you from finding a partner in the 'real world'.

CASE STUDY

Marie was an ardent fan of Victoria and David Beckham (Posh and Becks) – famous singer from The Spice Girls and England footballer. She read any magazines with their story in, watched TV programmes about the couple, and attended concerts that Victoria sang in. When their baby son was born, she sent a card of congratulation. Marie often fantasised about finding her own David Beckham look-alike and always looked for men that resembled him when she went to clubs with her friends. Part of the attraction was that they seemed to have a happy relationship. Marie's parents had broken up when she was ten. Marie had witnessed plenty of parental conflict from a young age, and so her dream was to find a relationship where this conflict would be absent. In searching for a Beckham clone of her own, she was really looking for the security that Posh and Becks seemed to represent.

Your influences – a personal profile

Now that you have given some thought to the different influences you may have encountered, use the following table to create a personal profile of some of the key influences on how you think about relationships. Tick the corresponding box to each statement under different subjects to help you reflect on particular issues. Try to do this as quickly as possible because in this way your unconscious thoughts and influences will rise to the surface, allowing you to uncover some surprises about how you approach particular issues.

Subject	Agree	Disagree
Money		
Couples should always share their financial concerns.		
It is important to save for a rainy day.		
You should live for today rather than tomorrow.		
It is OK to keep some part of a salary as a secret.		
A sound financial footing is crucial to a long-term relationship.		
Money is not important. How you feel about each other is the most important thing.		
If the woman earns more than the man he will feel emasculated.		

Subject	Agree	Disagree
In a long-term relationship it is best if both partners have a career of their own.		
On a first date, the man should always pay for the woman.		
I see myself as the kind of person who plans their spending.		
Communication		
It is important to talk about everything from day one of a new relationship.		
Sharing all your feelings and emotions is over-rated.		
I find it easy to talk to others.		
Least said, soonest mended.		
If you are really close to someone, you do not need words to share your feelings.		
Listening is as important as talking.		
Sometimes too many conversations can just confuse the issue you are trying to discuss.		
Men find it harder than women to talk about important concerns.		
A hug or a kiss can sometimes communicate important feelings.		

Subject	Agree	Disagree
Talking is easy if you love the person you are talking to.		
Most arguments occur because people do not listen properly in the first place.		
The main object of most rows is to get your own way.		
Frequent arguments indicate a serious relationship problem.		
If you argue with a partner at least it shows you care enough to debate an issue.		
Good communication allows for win/win results, rather than win/lose outcomes.		
Children		
It is important for a couple to plan together when they will have children.		
Children help to make a relationship stronger.		
Most people want children in their life.		
The arrival of children in a relationship can be a real stumbling block for many couples.		
If an accidental pregnancy occurs most people quickly come to terms with what has happened.		

Subject	Agree	Disagree
Children should be seen and not heard.		
Children need plenty of praise and affection in order to develop successfully.		
Babies should follow a strict schedule of care.		
Babies should be fed on demand.		
Children need two parents to care for them.		
It is selfish not to have children.		
Both partners in a relationship should share childcare in an equal fashion.		
Family and friends		
It is crucial to like one another's friends if you are to build a good relationship.		
Loving each other is the most important thing. Family opposition to a relationship is irrelevant.		
It is important to maintain independent friendships outside of the relationship.		
It is only to be expected that individuals will lose contact with friends once a new relationship is established.		

Subject	Agree	Disagree
It is important to create a good relationship with a partner's family, especially their parents.		
Without the support of family and friends, many relationships crumble.		
The most important thing is that the couple decide what they want from their relationship – the opinions of family and friends are much less important.		
If you ask your partner to end a friendship, they should do so for your sake.		
A partner should take your side in any dispute with family members, regardless of what the problem is.		

Once you have filled in the questionnaire, look back at your answers. Are there any surprises? Do you feel it accurately reflects some of your expectations and hopes for relationships? Has it also pointed out some of the key messages that your upbringing gave you about creating and maintaining relationships? It is also useful to reflect on what gave you the messages you feel you believe in. For example, you may have agreed with the statement about maintaining independent friends in the *Family and friends* section. Where has this idea come from? Did it come from reading a magazine that extolled the virtues of doing this, or from your father who has always kept up with his circle of friends from school days. As you read the next section look back at your answers to the questionnaire. Use your findings to help you think about what is still important to you in creating a new relationship, and what might need to be jettisoned before you think about entering a new partnership.

Your questionnaire responses

Money

This issue comes up as the number one argument topic for couples all over the UK. A Relate survey has shown that 40 per cent of couples rate money as the chief cause of difficulties. Many of these arguments stem from people coming together who have completely different agendas concerning finance. How you use money, and what it means to you, can have a serious impact on a new relationship, for good or ill. Some obvious examples might be the couple where one is a saver and the other a spendthrift. Sometimes this combination can cause fireworks because neither partner can come to terms with the attitude of the other. Occasionally, the saver will curb the spendthrift or the spendthrift will help the saver to loosen up a little so they can enjoy their savings. As you look back at your responses in this section, think about what your answers tell you. For instance, do you think you plan and save, or live for today? Could this change if you entered a long-term relationship? Do you have fixed ideas about how men and women should behave concerning money? Many of these ideas will have come from your family upbringing, so consider if your family messages on money still have a role, or if you feel they are not appropriate for your age or circumstances. For instance, you may have been brought up to believe that women should not earn more than men, but, as you follow your chosen career, this attitude may be preventing you from making a successful relationship.

Communication

Ask any couple counsellor or therapist what the chief difficulty that they encounter is and nine times out of ten they will say 'communication difficulties'. This is a huge 'umbrella' of an issue, covering everything from frequent arguments to talking about sex. At its most basic, good communication is about talking and listening to your partner. Listening is an overlooked art – most people imagine that talking to someone is enough. But good communication comes in three stages – talking and sharing, listening and attending, followed by appropriate action that follows up the discussion. As you reflect on your answers to this section, think about what informed the answers you gave. For example, you may have a close friend who went through a messy divorce and who has told you never to give all of yourself away too quickly, so that 'it is important to talk about everything . . .' seems like a bad idea. Or your family may have found discussing emotional issues difficult, telling you that 'least said, soonest mended' is an excellent axiom to live by if you want to avoid family fall-outs. Good communication is at the core of most relationships, so it is important to sort out what you want from your partner. Some of your decisions may also be coloured by your gender. More women than men seem to gravitate towards 'talking things through', but this is gradually changing as we become more emotionally literate in society. If you are a woman, perhaps you have received the idea that men do not willingly talk about their feelings or ideas and so you tend to take on this role in relationships. If you are a man, you may find your partner's talking distracting and annoying rather than enlightening. Thinking through your attitudes, and their origins, can help you decide the kind of communication you feel comfortable with and whether you want to make changes in this area of your life.

Children

It may seem a bit premature to think about your attitudes to becoming a parent at the start of a book on finding a partner, but this is one of the up and coming concerns for couples and individuals in modern life. Not only is there the issue of contraception (important right from the start of a relationship), but there is also the need to decide whether a career should take precedence over a family and whether an individual wants children at all. Although questions about becoming a parent may not be among the first you ask a potential partner, if the relationship becomes more serious, you can be sure that parenting concerns will come to the surface. If you have some idea of what you believe, and where that belief has come from, you will be able to talk about children in a more informed, and probably less heated, way. For instance, it may be that your parents are really looking forward to becoming grandparents. If they begin to drop big hints about producing a grandchild from the first day you move in with a partner then thinking about the responses to the questionnaire, and sharing your thoughts with your partner, will help you to weather the pressure you may feel from them. Alternatively, if you never want to have children, it is important that your partner knows this early on in the relationship. You may also 'inherit' step-children or meet your partner's children more quickly than you anticipated. If this is the case it is crucial that you have thought through what your approach might be. For instance, if you tend to think that 'children should be seen and not heard' you may have a big shock if your partner's children are noisy and demanding, causing conflict for the two of you just as you are trying to establish a new couple relationship. You may also find it helpful to think through your attitude to accidental pregnancy as this can sometimes be an extremely difficult issue for a new couple to cope with, especially if they have not even decided whether they wish to develop a commitment to one another.

Family and friends

Your attitude to the influence of your family and friends on your relationship can make or break that relationship. Many couples feel they are right for one another, but find they cannot cope with the reaction of friends or family to their liaison. The approval of a special friend can make a relationship seem perfect, while criticism by a parent can cause one or both partners to question what had previously seemed a happy partnership. Some obvious examples of this are when parents disapprove of their children making a relationship with someone who is of a different religious or ethnic background – a Jewish man wishing to marry a non-Jewish woman, for example. It is not unusual for a couple to believe that they can stand together against the storm of disapproval from friends or family – 'love will keep us together' – only to discover down the road that the withdrawal of support leads to stressful interactions with the chosen partner and a feeling that the relationship is built on sand rather than rock. All relationships take place within the structures of the communities we live in. You may think you can buck this system, but it takes a special kind of commitment to stay together when everyone you know thinks you should not be. Look back at your questionnaire to identify issues that might come up when you start a new relationship. For example, you may find that you have ticked the boxes which suggest that you expect your potential partner to give up their friends to spend time with you. Is this something you feel about a particular relationship? Does your attitude come from a situation where you felt jealous of a partner who seemed to prefer their friends to you?

Challenging personal values

Now you have completed the questionnaire and read about the different ways in which you may have formed your ideas about relationships, you may find that you would like to make some changes to these fundamental beliefs or feelings. You might feel this for a variety of reasons. For instance, you might have found yourself surprised by your answers, or shocked that you still believe something that you would like to think you have moved on from.

Here is how you can challenge these ideas and begin to construct new ways of thinking about money, communication, children, and family and friends from a relationship point of view:

- *Why do I want to change this way of thinking?*
  You may find it useful to make a list of why you are unhappy with a particular mind set. For instance, Erica was amazed to find that she ticked the 'agree' box in the communication section that said 'Most arguments are about getting your own way.' She had always seen herself as the kind of person who was willing to listen to her partner and to work on shared goals. She did not like the idea that she essentially used rows to score points from her partner. Choose possible changes that

genuinely relate to your desire to change, rather than make changes to try and please other people.

- **What is the possible outcome of changing this view of relationships?**
  You may want to make changes to your views, but you need to assess whether making a sudden change will impact on other parts of your life. Gita ticked the 'agree' box in the *Family and friends* section that suggested that the couple should take priority over family and friends. She knew that this went against her culture and the beliefs of her family, and that she had been influenced by the country she had been raised in (the UK) as opposed to the Asian country that her parents came from. She recognised that although she had developed new ways of thinking about couple relationships, any changes she made would need to be tackled in a slow and steady manner if she was to avoid her parents' anger or sadness.

- **When could you make this change?**
  It is important to assess when you will act on your discoveries from the questionnaire. You may decide that your family's view of how a couple spend their money is not helpful, and decide to change as soon as you find a new partner. But it may be useful to begin to put some changes in place before you meet someone new. For example, Fred came from a family who spent every penny they earned almost as soon as it arrived in the home. They were very happy with this, but Fred thought that it had often led to tough times when his parents were out of work. After his previous long-term relationship had broken up, partly as a result of lack of money, he decided to put some cash aside in order to feel more secure when he began dating again.

- **How will you implement the change you have chosen?**
  It is easy to identify changes you wish to make, but then find that your resolution fails when it comes to deciding how to actually get something to work. Lucy felt this when she found

that she ticked the 'agree' box under the *Family and friends* section against the statement about liking one another's friends in order to build a happy relationship. Throughout their five-year marriage, Lucy had been involved in a running battle with her ex-husband regarding his friends. She had not liked them, and forbade them to come to the house. Lucy knew she never wanted to face this situation again, and decided that she would try to meet any friends of a new partner quickly to give her a chance of building a relationship with them as well as with a potential partner.

You may find that you are happy about some of the boxes you have chosen as they reveal someone who has a healthy attitude to creating new relationships. You may have ticked the 'agree' box against the statement, 'It is important to talk about everything from day one of a new relationship', because you regard yourself as an open person who is willing to share feelings and ideas with another. Or you may feel pleased that you regard yourself as the kind of person who plans their spending. Whatever you have identified as positive, be proud that you value this part of yourself. Later in the book you will find more information about creating the basic building blocks of relationships with a new partner.

In conclusion

This chapter has introduced the context of the modern relationship and outlined the importance of couple relationships, despite many changes to relationship styles in recent years. In addition you have looked at the general influences on couple relationships, and on individuals as they contemplate making new partnerships. You have been asked to complete a personal values questionnaire and you have thought about how to make challenges to long-held, and now inappropriate, beliefs about couple relationships.

2

What Kind of Relationship Do You Want?

If you want to get to grips with what you want or need from a relationship, you need to begin by understanding a bit more about yourself. You may have found that, in the past, you have been drawn to a certain kind of person, or found yourself in a situation that you told yourself you would never end up in again. In this chapter you will learn more about yourself and what kind of relationship suits you, as well as the way in which different character types complement each other.

Who are you?

In Chapter One you have already begun to make sense of how you approach relationships by answering a questionnaire on differing attitudes to a variety of issues. This next questionnaire is designed to help you recognise how you respond to particular situations, while also helping you to learn more about your personality and character.

Circle the answer that most accurately describes how you think you would behave in a given situation. It is unlikely that you will find an exact match because everyone tends to react differently to

28

events, so just choose the answer that approximates to your usual behaviour.

---

1 While out with friends for a quiet drink at a local pub, a girl is pestered by a drunk. She is embarrassed, and the drunk does not seem to know when to take no for an answer. You:

A make a joke of the situation and suggest moving on to another pub.

B watch to see what other members of the group do in response to the situation.

C ask the pub landlord to ban the drunk.

D tell the girl you will protect her.

E demand that the pub landlord take action and tell everyone to leave.

---

2 Your workmate tells you in strictest confidence that she is expecting a baby. She wants this news to be confidential as she is not sure how the boss will respond. Soon after, you discover that a colleague has also heard the news and told the boss. You:

A tell the colleague that she has caused a problem.

B decide it has little to do with you.

C ask the personnel department for information on expectant mothers' rights at work.

D tell your workmate that the boss will be delighted to hear about the baby. Doesn't everyone love babies?

E immediately tell the boss that they must treat your workmate with absolute fairness.

---

3 You are out shopping when you notice that a builder's ladder is placed so dangerously it could fall and cause an accident. You:

A find the builder and politely ask him to move the ladder.

B ignore the ladder, but worry about it all the way home on the bus.

C move the ladder yourself.

D   move the ladder, and imagine all the accidents you have prevented.

E   tackle the builder in a fairly aggressive way about his carelessness.

4   You and your partner both work. When you return from work, he or she has hardly ever started to cook an evening meal. This causes arguments, during which your partner states that he/she thinks it is your job. You:

A   point out that you both have the same workload.

B   suggest a take-away.

C   draw up a rota so that you take turns to cook the meal throughout the week.

D   suggest looking for a home help, even if you really know this is too expensive.

E   demand that they see things your way, and tell them it is their job to cook the evening meal.

5   Your sister tells you that her marriage has hit a rough patch and she suspects her husband of having an affair. You:

A   tell her she can come and stay with you, although you know your partner should be told first.

B   say you cannot believe he would do such a thing.

C   ask her if she has any unequivocal proof that he is having an affair.

D   suggest that if she ignores it he will probably end the affair soon.

E   find her husband and ask for an explanation of what is going on.

6   You and your partner are choosing a holiday. You:

A   describe exactly the kind of holiday you want this year.

B   wait until your partner says what they want and then agree, even if it is not precisely what you had in mind.

C   find a holiday venue that will allow you both to follow the leisure pursuits you enjoy.

D   make a list of all the holiday ideas you have ever had.

E   organise a surprise holiday and whisk your partner away.

7   You and your partner are watching a TV debate show. Your partner unexpectedly sides with the person you think is wrong. You:

A   argue that they are misguided, but do not take the situation too seriously.

B   keep quiet about your beliefs.

C   ask your partner to explain why they agree with the opposing side.

D   tell yourself and/or your partner that you cannot really believe what they are saying.

E   tell them they are wrong and explain why in detail.

8   Your family decide to get together to celebrate Christmas. You know that there can be conflict between your brother and father. You:

A   take your father aside and tell him you are worried about what will happen if he and your brother spend time together.

B   decide to keep out of any problems by only visiting for a short time.

C   talk to your brother about the problem and suggest ways of managing the potential difficulty.

D   hope that the spirit of Christmas will eliminate the difficulties.

E   organise a meeting between your father and brother to thrash things out.

9   It is the anniversary of your partner's mother's death. You:

A   take them out for a meal to cheer them up.

B   decide not to mention it in case it raises more sadness.

C   send them a bouquet of flowers with a kind note attached.

D   tell them their mum is 'at peace' and they should not grieve any longer.

E   talk about their mum, which makes them cry, and then say that a good weep is a beneficial part of the mourning process.

10 You want to buy a car. You:

A tour the local car showrooms to talk to the different sales staff about each model.

B pore over the brochures on the models you think you might like.

C make a list of the pros and cons of each model.

D buy motoring magazines and change your mind about each car as you read each new feature.

E go to a number of car showrooms and ask for details on finance arrangements and possible deals they may have available.

---

11 Your local hospice is recruiting new volunteers. You are not sure if you want to help and so attend an open evening. As the evening goes on you find you are still not sure. You:

A explain at the end of the evening that you are not ready to make up your mind.

B sneak out of the back of the room before anyone can speak to you.

C ask for leaflets and further information to take away so that you can make a decision.

D agree to help, seeing yourself holding the hands of dying people, even though you know this might be tough.

E tell the organiser that you think they should pay for the services of volunteers.

Mostly As

You are an outgoing and probably extrovert person. You tend to speak your mind without worrying too much about the effect on others, although you are not insensitive and are capable of tailoring your remarks to a given situation. You usually get your information from other people – by asking for an opinion, by making observations or in discussion – rather than by reading instruction books, for instance. You have a wide circle of friends, but may not have a 'special' friend with whom you share intimacies. You are well known for getting on with most people, and you are not shy of meeting new groups of people. It is possible that you have an impulsive streak that sometimes causes you to make decisions you later regret, but this spontaneity may mean you can also grasp good opportunities that come your way. Occasionally, you may make a joke, or avoid thinking through a serious situation, so that others may feel you have missed the main point of a situation, or wonder if you have failed to grasp the real issue at stake.

As an extrovert you often pick partners from the following categories:

- A partner who is like you and who can also relate easily to groups of people. This kind of person may not be big on emotional involvement, so that your relationship always has a relaxed and slightly 'open' feel to it. They may be a member of your group of friends, so that the relationship feels less intense than one with someone previously a stranger.
- A partner who is the opposite to your extrovert personality – perhaps shyer and less talkative (see B type people below). You may seek this kind of partnership because you need the balance that this kind of person can give to your life, especially if you are looking for relief from always playing the 'life and soul' of the party.
- A partner who is very practical (see C type people below). This kind of partner can supply an emotional anchor, allowing you to feel safe because they will support you with their straightforward approach to life.

Mostly Bs

You are a quiet and fairly introverted person. This does not mean you do not enjoy social gatherings, but they may feel quite stressful because you find it difficult to spontaneously strike up conversation. You are likely to think things through at length, but avoid discussing your thinking with others. Sometimes this aspect of your character leads you to worry, turning concerns over and over in your mind. You may avoid taking speedy action on issues, but this can be of benefit because you often formulate a full picture of all the sides to a problem or decision. Your quietness may be misinterpreted by others as implying that you are 'boring', but the truth is that still waters often do run deep, so it may be a matter of seeking friends who understand your true depths, rather than trying to be more outgoing in order to fit in. You may also be a bit of an 'avoider' – that is you tend to avoid problems rather than face them head on. In some situations this can be a positive as you avoid the knee-jerk responses of those around you who rush into situations, only to regret their behaviour at a later date.

As an introvert you often pick a partner from the categories below:

- A partner who is more outgoing than yourself. Opposites often attract because they tend to compensate for the missing parts of each other – the loud, talkative man who links up with a quiet, shy woman, for example. These relationships can work on the principle that the two different, but equal, halves make a whole. However, they can also run into trouble because what seemed attractive becomes annoying – perhaps the loud man wants a woman to party with, not a 'mouse' who sits in the corner.
- A partner who is demanding and controlling (see E type people below). It is a bit of a puzzle as to why B types are attracted to E types, but it may be because they often protect a shy person from the big, bad world, albeit by censoring their behaviour and activities. Their protection can seem like caring at the start of such a relationship. It may only be after some time that the B type person feels they are in a gilded cage.
- A partner who is highly practical and sensible (see C type people below). If you are a B type personality, you may lack confidence and so be attracted to those people who seem to find it easy to make decisions and who run their lives on well-oiled tracks.

Mostly Cs

You are a practical down-to-earth type who can always be relied upon to work out a sensible arrangement when others are running around like headless chickens. Occasionally, others may feel you lack a little romance or mystery, but most people are only too happy to look to your expert planning or useful advice when needed. You may not always find it easy to enter into jokes or act impulsively, and this can prevent you from being very outgoing. But you are usually extremely loyal and once a friend will stay a friend. You are a little in danger of being taken for granted by others, or put upon, because of your ability to sort out messes. You are usually a good listener because you like to gather all the facts about a situation before taking action. You may find it hard to understand creative people because they often appear to do things that are not underscored by strategy and decision, but you are prepared to try to make sense of things that seem alien to you at first sight.

As a practical person you often pick a partner from the categories below:

- You may be attracted to people who are shy or quieter than most. This is because they may raise less protest over your careful plans than more impulsive types, and because they probably appeal to your considered approach to life.
- In the vein of opposites attracting, you may feel a strange pull towards people who are dreamers and slightly unworldly (see type D people below). You may unconsciously feel that they balance your 'feet on the ground' approach, and, at some levels, you even look forward to their wacky ideas!
- You could be tempted to team up with a 'control freak' (see type E people below) because they could represent a challenge, and they might feel an attraction to your rational lifestyle as it does not have the uncertainties of a partner constantly challenging their desire to control.

Mostly Ds

You are one of life's incurable romantics! You tend to see the best in people and have dreams about the kind of person you would like to be. You may not be the most sensible of people, given to impulsive choices and behaviour, but you can be a lot of fun to be with. Most romantics are optimists, always seeing the rainbow around the corner, even if storm clouds are gathering overhead. There is a danger that you will eventually lose your romanticism when the real world intrudes on your idyll. Joni Mitchell, singer and songwriter, says 'All romantics meet the same fate/someday cynical . . . boring someone in some dark café,' and there may be some truth in this vision of the person who has once lived on dreams but has now crashed to earth. Romantics are often warm and affectionate people who are capable of close friendships and can help people to dream dreams about their future. Although they are usually non-realists, they can sometimes have powerful and intuitive feelings about other people and situations.

As a romantic you often pick a partner from the categories below:

- You are probably attracted to people who are good at inter-acting with others and willing to maintain a wide circle of friends (see type A people above). You probably enjoy this kind of link because it gives you the chance to hear about the lives of others and to imagine schemes that might develop these friendships for other reasons – perhaps in work, for instance.

- Practical people may also be your type as they will help to keep you grounded (see type C people above). The old cliché about opposites attracting is particularly true for this kind of alliance and will bring benefits to both of you. Your practical partner can help you to engage with the realities of modern life, while you can add a little fun to theirs.

- You may also be familiar with the partnership where you end up doing what your partner tells you rather than feeling you have an equal partnership (see E type people below). Your romantic streak may cause you to see this kind of person as seductive because they seem to have life 'sewn-up' in a way that you do not. You may often have fallen for this kind of person after a failed love affair with a fellow dreamer. After a relationship between two dreamers, where there was little fixed and steady behaviour, being with someone who appeared to take control was a welcome relief.

Mostly Es

I am afraid it has to be said, you are a bit of a control freak! You tend to like things to go your own way and you can be extremely assertive. If you can combine this side of your character with a willingness to listen to and care for others your tough stance can be extremely attractive. If, however, you use this side of yourself to try to get what you want at the expense of others, it can be a destructive influence on relationships. You may think you are demonstrating a caring side by taking charge of travel plans or sorting out a work problem, but you should consider what your partner is really looking for rather than simply barging in with your own ideas. That said, you are a steadfast friend who always wants to see the best in others, and will be the first to leap to their defence in a difficult situation. You probably have a strong sense of right and wrong, and possess scrupulous ideas about what is acceptable and what is not. Other people may sometimes find you rather unnerving, especially if you weigh in with your opinions in a forceful way, but you are not often aware of this quality in yourself.

As a forceful character, you often pick a partner from the categories below:

- A quiet or rather shy person (see type B above). This is either because you feel better in control with someone who does not challenge you or because you want to protect someone who may seem less able to stand up for themselves.
- A practical person who has their feet on the ground. This kind of person may be attractive because you feel comfortable around someone who can add good planning to your dogged determination to achieve a goal once you have set your heart on it.
- You may be drawn to a fellow E type person, but this is not always a marriage made in heaven. You may find that you argue, or try to control each other so that the relationship feels tense and uncomfortable.

You may have discovered, through completing this questionnaire, that you are a mixture of several different types, or that you have been a different person in different relationships. Sometimes you may have been content to sit in the background and allow your partner to take centre stage. At other times, you may have wanted to be in control of the situation. Each new relationship will draw out of you different facets of behaviour, emphasising different parts of your character. This is normal, and you may have noticed the same phenomenon at work or when you are out with friends. You will probably also have noticed changes in your approach to relationships through ageing or because of different life experiences. In other words, what you want from a relationship is affected by the circumstances in which you find yourself. If you are generally a quiet person, you may sometimes want to be brought out of yourself, or sometimes want to be left alone.

Understanding self-perception

How we perceive ourselves is important when thinking about making new relationships. It is likely that our self-perception is different, at least in some ways, to the perception others have of us.

CASE STUDY

Lorna received an invitation to a school reunion. It was twenty years since she had seen the other people from her school, and she felt very nervous as she posted the reply slip to the woman organising the reunion. Lorna had never thought much of herself at school – she had been poor at sports, something that was prized at the school, and she did not do stunningly well in exams. But Lorna had a special talent. She was a singer in a local Country & Western bar, often working with a band that held line-dancing classes. She did this in her spare time, but her interest in singing dated back to her schooldays when she had once sung a solo in a school concert. On the day of the reunion, she arrived at the school hall feeling very mixed about being there. To her intense surprise a man she hardly recognised, but who had been a member of her class, greeted her warmly and found her a seat. Lorna fell into conversation with others around her, and was chatting happily when the man, Ian, returned.

He said, 'I was really hoping you would come tonight. I wanted to tell you what an impression that solo you sang at the school concert made on me all those years ago. I thought you were really brave. I could never do anything like that.'

Lorna was amazed. Ian had been a bit of a football star in his year, and had hardly ever held a conversation with her when she was sixteen. She was even more surprised when he said that he remembered and liked the song so much that he had had it played at his wedding! Lorna went on to tell the others about her Country & Western music, and felt they really enjoyed hearing about her singing success.

How we perceive ourselves can be completely at odds with the way in which others see us. Lorna had seen herself as bit of an outsider at school. Not interested in sport, and no genius at exams, she thought that everyone at the school would have forgotten all about her. To discover that Ian saw things very differently was a complete eye-opener. Lorna found that she viewed herself differently as a result of learning that her rather self-critical view was not necessarily the same as the view that others had of her.

Your physical self

Perhaps the most common area in which self-perception can really affect the relationships we make is that relating to how we feel about our body and its functioning. For instance, if you were teased at school about being over or underweight, if you felt very self-conscious about your breast size or lack of muscle in your teens or if a previous partner has criticised some part of your body, you may find that you lack confidence in your body and avoid intimate contact. Some people try to hide parts of their body in lovemaking for instance, but this usually makes sex very difficult and lacking in spontaneity. You may just feel awkward about socialising, wondering if your figure will fit in with the crowd – perhaps you think you are too thin, too fat, too tall, too short etc. This feeling can be very acute in the teens and twenties, but often returns if you are going back to dating after a divorce or relationship break-up.

Boosting physical self-esteem

If you feel you need a little help in feeling more confident about your body, here are some ideas:

- Love your body as it is now. It is not unusual for people to postpone the enjoyment of going out and meeting others by saying, 'I'll start clubbing/visiting friends/having a drink at the pub when I have lost this extra weight.' This kind of prevarication can occur if you have been hurt by a previous relationship, and it may not all be related to your body size. But if you can grow to accept yourself as you are today, you will find your confidence will grow. If you feel uncomfortable about your image, buy clothes that really fit well (rather than trying to squash into the size you were years ago!) and buy the best grooming products you can afford. Have your hair done and tell yourself you are as good as anyone else – because you are!

- The old adage 'you are what you eat' has some truth in it. If you want a healthy body that can get you through the stresses and strains of modern life, you need to eat proper food. Eat five portions of fruit and vegetables a day and avoid foods rich in fats and sugar. Of course, you have probably heard or read this kind of advice before – whole industries have been built on it – but it is true that the better you eat, the better you will feel. Food high in fat can induce feelings of lethargy, while sugary foods may give you an instant high, but then produce an energy slump that leaves you feeling hungry again. If you really want to lose weight (and it is important that this decision is taken for yourself, not just to please someone else, or to conform to an impossibly thin, model-like image) then try a slimming group. Everyone else is in the same boat, and you will receive friendly help and support to get you to your goal.

- Take regular exercise. Again, I am sure you have read or heard this a hundred times, but regular exercise can really help you to feel good about yourself. Exercise releases feel-good chemicals into the brain, and can improve how you perceive your body. The latest thinking on exercise is that you require short doses of exercise every day, rather than one or two longer bouts in the week. Ten to twenty minutes each day of something you enjoy – such as walking, swimming, dancing, gardening, or jogging – can help to keep your muscles, bones and heart strong. Although you may want to join a gym, and this can be very good for you, you do not actually have to go to this expense. Walking or jogging in your local park, running up and down your stairs at home or using a reputable exercise video can all help you to achieve a daily dose of exercise.

- A good friend of mine once told me to 'be proud of the space you occupy'. I think she is right – whatever your size or shape, if you can feel proud of yourself, you will feel proud of your body.

Your social self

Some people seem to manage to feel confident in any social situation. They can talk with ease to anyone and fit in well in most groups. But most of us find that we sometimes feel confident about socialising and at other times feel nervous and unsure about meeting others. If you are one of the people who finds it excruciatingly difficult to meet and talk to people, life must sometimes seem very hard. If you feel you could do with some help to improve your social skills, or brush up those you already feel reasonably confident about, here are some tips:

Improving social self-esteem

- If you find that conversation dries up quickly when you meet new people, ask lots of questions (but avoid interrogating the other person!). They will talk to you and you can respond with your own information because they will probably ask you questions in return. Try not to ask 'what do you do' as this might give the impression you are only interested in their work. (This does happen a lot, however, at 'networking' type parties, where it is probably acceptable.) Instead, ask about their interests, reading habits, the latest films they have enjoyed and so on. This approach will give you lots of information about the person you are talking to which will help you to develop the conversation.

- Avoid standing in a corner. Choose a place where people are coming and going – a buffet table or drinks corner can be good as you can engage individuals in conversation about the delicious pudding or offer to pour a drink. But beware of spending the entire time at these venues or your fellow guests might think you are a glutton or a drunk! Once you have spoken to a few people, move around the room and talk to those with whom you have already made contact.

- Compliment people on something you like – perhaps an item of their clothing, the picture they have on the wall or their lovely garden. Remember, this must be genuine or you will sound completely insincere, and nothing puts people off like insincerity. They will probably respond by telling you all about where they bought it or the work they put in to create it. This will get the conversation flowing.

- If you are really nervous in a large crowd, try hosting a dinner party, with at least half the invitees being people you already know well. You do not need to go mad on expensive food or spend hours cooking – you could even cheat with some ready-made Marks & Spencer food! The object is to develop confidence in meeting people and talking easily, rather than to serve a cordon bleu meal. If this sounds a bit too much, try a simple supper of special bread, cheese and salad with some exotic desserts. You can serve this kind of meal on a coffee table or as a buffet. If you really feel you cannot manage the preparation, ask people round for a take-away pizza or a curry. The object is to get used to relating to groups, so any excuse will do.

- Avoid people you really feel you do not get on with. This might sound obvious – who mixes with people they do not like? Well, lots of us do. We may do this because we fear that if we do not go out with a particular crowd we will be left socially high and dry. Or we may feel slightly bullied into always being with the same person or group. A variation on this can occur in work relationships where you feel you have to keep 'in' with the group in your office or on your floor for fear of being ostracised if you do not, and that this will affect your job. But the truth is that if you make yourself spend time with people you do not admire or with whom you find it hard to converse, you will eventually feel lonely and lacking in support. You might even develop a false image of yourself that is hard to shake off – that you want and need people who talk you into drinking heavily or that you feel comfortable bitching about others behind their backs. If you feel you have got into the wrong crowd, look for interests that will allow you to meet like-minded people. For instance, you might join a local cinema society or local walkers' club.

Your emotional self

Do you feel you conceal your emotions? Or that they are sometimes too much on show? Many people struggle with keeping their emotions under control because they fear that showing how they feel will place a barrier between them and the person they are with. Others find it hard to show feeling at all, and that this is a handicap when dealing with people. Showing emotion appropriate to the moment and circumstances is a balancing act. The idea that we should have our emotions on show all the time seems to have gained currency in recent years, probably as a result of the spread of therapy and counselling. In fact, while it may be OK to show emotion in the context of counselling, to adopt this stance in everyday life would end up with most of us feeling very unhappy indeed. Imagine bawling out your neighbour because of their practice of mowing the lawn every Sunday morning, or declaring undying love to your daughter's teacher when you clapped eyes on them at a PTA meeting! It is obvious that part of the maturing process is gaining control of emotion and allowing it to be displayed at appropriate times. There is as much of a problem with inappropriately repressed emotion as there is with letting it all hang out. If you cannot offer praise, give a hug, weep with someone when it is right to do so, then you will live a very sterile life. What you may feel is too much or too little emotion may seem completely different to another. A good example of this is when a parent responds to their child showing them a painting. You might remember a similar scenario from childhood. To the adult some constructive remark, such as 'the tree is too big', may only be intended to offer some help in painting accurately. To the child, it may feel like a slight, that their parent does not see the importance of the painting. It is not possible to always get the emotional balancing act exactly right, but here are some ideas to help you work on building emotional self-esteem:

Building emotional self-esteem

- When you want to express feeling, begin your sentences or statements with, 'I feel . . .'. You will find that this causes two things to happen. Firstly, you will register what you really do feel. Is it really anger or could it be sadness, frustration or shock, for instance. Secondly, if you are trying to communicate your feelings to another, they will know that what you are saying is your response and you are not holding them responsible for your feelings.

- If you have got stuck in a groove of always responding to events in just one way – with anger, tears or silence, for example – ask yourself if this is helping or hindering your relationships. Consider if your emotional 'one note' is allowing you to express what you really feel you need to express.

- Ask other people what they are feeling about a particular event. For example, Kelly found it hard to relate to the response of other parents when their children acted in the school Christmas play. She noticed that many parents were clearly very moved, whereas she felt anxious in case her son made a mistake. After the play, she talked to three friends, asking them to share what they had been feeling. They described the mix of pride, excitement and love that overwhelmed them and this helped Kelly to be more in touch with the way in which emotion worked in other people. Listening to other people in this way can help you to develop an emotional repertoire that feels right for you.

- It is not unusual for partners, family and friends to tell you what you should, or should not, be feeling. For instance, Mike was very upset when his dog died. He had looked after his dog since puppyhood and as he lived alone with her, he felt a real sense of bereavement when she died of old age. When he phoned his sister to tell her the sad news, she responded by telling him to 'stop sounding so miserable – it was only a dog'. Mike was initially upset at his sister's remarks, but then found himself wondering if he was making too much of his feelings. The fact is that if you feel the feeling, it is real to you. What you decide to do with the emotion is another matter. You may decide to tell lots of people how you are feeling, or only those who you know will be sympathetic to what you are going through (and perhaps Mike would have been well advised to avoid his sister until he felt more able to cope with her robust approach), or to keep the feeling to yourself. Some of these responses will be dictated by your circumstances, but nevertheless, whatever you feel is right for you should be treated with respect by others. Because other people do not respond in the same way as you does not make your experience less authentic.

Your mental self

If someone you know breaks their leg, it is easy to show sympathy. Their problem is obvious and is usually regarded as an accident, caused by outside forces, such as a slippery path. But mental health concerns are treated very differently. There is still, despite the fact that modern understanding about mental illness proves otherwise, the notion that you must have caused the illness yourself in an almost deliberate way and that all that is required is that you pull yourself together. Imagine saying this to the poor person lying in the street with a broken leg. We would be appalled to think that this could happen, but with mental health it happens every day. We find it embarrassing to empathise with the colleague who is off work with stress or to talk to a friend who has depression. Until recently this may have been because treatment for mental illness was patchy and somewhat experimental. But this is not the story now. Antidepressants, medicines for other problems, therapy, counselling and hospitalisation can all work wonders with mental illness. But our continuing reluctance to talk about mental illness or mental health problems can lead us to ignore the signs and symptoms of mental difficulties. We may even regard ourselves as weak for feeling stressed, depressed or anxious. If you want to protect or improve your mental state, here are some suggestions:

Improving mental health

- Make sure you build regular time into your day to relax and switch off from the demands of the day. Try to avoid watching too much TV or resorting to alcohol to do this for you as both are potentially stimulating rather than de-stressing. Instead, listen to soothing music or take a warm bath with plenty of oil or bubbles.

- Talk about your feelings to people you trust, as often as you can. Crushing your feelings, or allowing them to go round and round in your head, can lead to depression and a sense of futility. If you feel that things are really on top of you, try and arrange to talk things over with a counsellor.

- Exercise as regularly as you can. Exercise is a natural relaxant, and can allow you to get rid of the negative emotions that can lead to worry and anxiety.

- Seek the help of a GP if you feel you are not coping well with life. You may fear that you will 'just be given a tablet' but this is an unfounded fear. Many modern drugs are not habit forming and can get you through a bad patch if you need it. Your GP will also be able to advise you on self-help groups in your locality that could help you with particular problems, or refer you to a surgery counsellor as many surgeries now have this facility.

Your ideal relationship

Now that you have gained a little more understanding about yourself and your personality from the exercises above, and begun to think about the kind of partner you have often found yourself with in the past, this section will help you to think about what qualities you want in a relationship. Later in the book we will consider the kind of partner you may wish to meet, but for now it is OK to be a little idealistic and imagine the kind of partnership you would want in an ideal world. You may not find this perfect love, but sometimes it is important to start any project with a vision. If you do this now it is possible to refine it at a later stage. Remember President Kennedy's famous speech about 'putting a man on the moon'? He did not go on to tell the expectant crowd in great detail how this was to be achieved. Instead, he presented the vision, and NASA worked on the detail! This is what I am asking you to do now. Think of your vision of the kind of relationship you would like. It might help you to write down your personal answers to the questions in the categories listed below. I have chosen these because my experience in counselling has taught me that these are the areas that most people feel are important, but there is no reason why you should not list your own choices as well.

Category	Questions to ask yourself in this category
Trust	How important is trust to you? Do you want to feel you can place absolute trust in a partner, or would it be enough to trust them in particular areas, such as holding down a job, for instance? How would you define trust in a relationship?
Commitment	Would your ideal relationship be a long-term, for life, commitment? Or are you looking for a short-term relationship to suit your present situation? Do you want to marry, cohabit or simply 'go out' with someone?
Affection	Would you like a relationship where your partner is openly demonstrative? Or more reserved? Do you like to show affection?
Negotiation	Would you like a relationship where you negotiate everything? Or do you want a relationship where at least some of the decisions are taken by your partner unilaterally? (This might be important if you are from a particular religious background.)
Communication	Do you want a partner who talks to you about everything? Or do you prefer to just talk about issues when they arise? Do you think you are good at communicating? Or do you tend to rely on a partner to speak for you?

Category	Questions to ask yourself in this category
Shared interests	Are you looking for a partner who enjoys all the same things that you do? Or would you like a relationship where you do not necessarily share the same interests?
Similar cultural/ ethnic/religious background	It may be very important to you that your relationship is with someone who shares the same background as you, or you may prefer to meet someone who is different. (It could be important to consider the impact on your relationship if your family does not support your choice.)
Age similarity or difference	Would your ideal relationship be with someone of a similar age to you, older or younger? If you would like an age difference, roughly how great would this difference be?
Sexual compatibility	How important is sex in your life? Would you like a relationship that is sexual or could you tolerate a non-sexual relationship? Are you willing to contemplate changes to sexual compatibility over the length of a relationship?
Past relationships	Are you willing to have a relationship with someone who has had a previous committed relationship? For instance, how do you feel about becoming a step-parent? Or dealing with an ex-partner?
Work and home balance	Do you want a relationship where you both expect to work full time? Or do you expect that you (or your partner) will be the main breadwinner? Do you expect to share domestic tasks equally?
Other people	Do you want to have a lively social life? Or do you expect to have a quiet relationship with little interaction with others? Do you want to be close to a partner's family (and feel they are close to yours), or would you like some distance in this area?

As you make notes under these various headings, you will find a pattern begins to emerge. For instance, Clare found that she had more ideas about what she wanted from a relationship than she expected. Some were quite surprising. She discovered that she would be happy with a relationship with an older man, would be ready to take on a partner's children, with support from him, and expected to maintain her own network of friends during any relationship. She also had strong feelings about wanting to ensure an equal share of domestic tasks and expected that any relationship would be faithful. Clare realised she wanted a long-term commitment, but not necessarily marriage.

Making a list of this kind, even when you feel that making a new relationship is a long way off, is useful for some important reasons:

- It will help you to avoid choosing relationships that seem attractive because there seems to be no one else you like more.
- You can discover what your widest parameters are for any potential relationship. For instance, you might be happy to put up with an older partner, but only if they were less than ten years older than you.
- You can challenge yourself if you want to change any of your previous thinking about how relationships should be. For example, you may think you want a lifelong relationship but could begin to consider something a little less committed in the short term.

A note on love

You may have been asking yourself where the magic word 'love' is in the categories described above. It is not that I do not think that love is very important in any relationship – of course love is crucial. But how we love, what makes us love one partner and not another, or what love means to us, is very individual to each person. I have chosen the categories above because when we are content with each of these areas I believe we can call this love. I am often asked for a definition of love and I usually say the following; it is not my original thought, but it seems to describe love: Love is when you have your needs met. Of course, some love is destructive – carrying on loving a violent man may mean that you risk being wounded by your love. But all love must mean that at some level you have your emotional needs met, or it is not really true love.

Keep the results of this exercise, along with your answers to previous questionnaires, somewhere safe. You can then use the answers to help you think through some of the issues that follow in the next few chapters. The object of all this self-reflection is to allow you to discover who you are, and what this means when you choose a partner, while helping you to make sense of the kind of relationship you think you might like. In the next chapter, you can learn more about how past experiences of relationships might have affected you and what to do to minimise negative effects while maximising those things you want to repeat in a new relationship.

In conclusion

This chapter has asked you to think about who you are and what influence this has on how to you choose the people you have relationships with.

In addition, you will have filled in a number of questionnaires about yourself and the kind of relationship you really want. You will have also read about understanding the importance of, or improving, your perception of your physical, social, emotional and mental self.

3

What Have I Learnt From Past Relationships?

When you read the title of this chapter, you might well have found yourself asking 'Why would I want to think about the past? It is what my future relationships will look like that I want to know about.' My answer is that you cannot really make a successful relationship in the future without considering what happened to you in previous relationships. This is because old assumptions or feelings that influenced you as you matured and developed relationships can hang around, often affecting new partnerships at an unconscious level.

Your emotional backpack

Here is an analogy to help you understand this idea. Imagine that all the things you have learnt about relationships from parents, friends, previous partners and other sources are like items of clothing you want to pack. At the start of your life, and as you grow, you gradually begin to put these items in a backpack that you carry around with you wherever you go. Sometimes these items feel heavy and uncomfortable (for example, if you feel guilty about a sexual relationship your parents disapprove of) or light and easy to carry (for instance, if you have a relationship that makes you very happy). All this stuff slowly fills the backpack as you travel. You take out the clothes to wear, discard some that feel too small or too shabby, and keep others for sentimental reasons. If the temperature gets hot, you buy cool clothes; if cold, you wrap up warm. Mostly you carry stuff around with you that you do not even know you have. In each new relationship you unpack some and include new things.

Your emotional backpack is stuffed with ideas you have gleaned from watching friends interact, remembering how you solved things with a previous partner, fantasising about the perfect lover and a million other issues that rarely make an appearance except sometimes in arguments, when your partner may point out to you that you are 'behaving irrationally' or may accuse you of treating him or her 'just like your last partner'. When you enter a new relationship, getting to grips with what you are carrying as a pack will considerably increase the chances of it succeeding. You can 'wash out' any ways of behaving that are inappropriate, 'throw out the rubbish' from other partnerships that have no place in what you have today, and preserve anything that is precious. This will also create room for new ideas and beliefs to enter the 'emotional backpack', allowing you to learn from these as you move through unknown 'relationship terrain'.

CASE STUDY

Jo met Craig some months after she had split up with her boyfriend of five years. Jo and Derek (her ex) had lived together for three years when Jo was shocked to discover that he had been seeing someone else for six months. In the aftermath of the revelation of the infidelity, Jo acted very swiftly, moving out of their shared flat and into a bedsit nearby. Derek asked her to stay, telling Jo that the girl he had been seeing was not 'very important' but Jo felt that all her trust had been broken. What made things worse was that this was not the first time that Jo had been through a break-up following an affair. Her previous boyfriend, whom she had met at university, had also had another girlfriend, whom she later married.

When Jo first met Craig, she was extremely wary of his interest. For some weeks she avoided seeing him at all, which was difficult because he was the brother of a good friend. But Craig found out her mobile phone number and left a message asking Jo to come for a drink with him. After some reflection Jo agreed, but spent most of the evening answering Craig in monosyllables. Craig wondered if he was getting the brush off, but despite this cool reception from Jo, he persevered because he felt that Jo probably had a much more open personality beneath the 'closed-up' Jo he was meeting. Several dates followed, but instead of Jo opening up, she seemed to close up even further. She was often late in meeting Craig and on a couple of occasions she stood him up. Craig found it hard to understand what he was doing wrong. He tried to be considerate and thoughtful towards Jo, but the nicer he was, the more Jo backed off.

Then one evening, after watching a weepy film at the local cinema, Jo and Craig found themselves in an almost deserted Chinese restaurant. Jo had a couple of glasses of wine and began to talk to Craig about her experiences with men. She told him all about Derek, and the previous student boyfriend. She also talked about her parents and in particular her father's problems with money, often brought on by gambling with cash the family could not afford to lose. It became clear to Craig that Jo had a serious problem trusting men. She obviously felt that men usually took advantage of women, and that it was the woman's role to keep them in line. Jo admitted that she had done this with Craig when she was either late or had not turned up for dates.

She said, 'I wanted to keep you guessing. Then you would be on your toes, and I had the upper hand. I never want to be at the beck and call again of a man who thinks I will put up with anything.'

Craig and Jo continued to go out together, but it took over a year before Jo seemed to relax a little with Craig. They eventually moved in together, but sometimes still argue when Jo appears to shut herself off from Craig.

The object of this case study is to show how previous relationships (and the observation of those of family and friends) can affect the start of a new partnership. Here are some of the things that are in Jo's backpack:

Mistrust

Jo has been hurt by three men in her life – her father, who often broke promises about not gambling; her student boyfriend, who not only took another girlfriend but went on to commit to her in a way he was unprepared to with Jo; and Derek, who had an affair behind her back.

Anxiety

Jo fears that no man will ever give her what she really wants – a loving and close relationship – and this causes her to vacillate between wanting a relationship, and wanting to avoid one.

A desire to be found attractive

The two major betrayals of her previous boyfriends have left Jo feeling that she must be unattractive if she can lose a partner so easily. Although she was nervous about Craig, she also wanted the lift to her self-esteem that his attention gave her.

Some feelings of revenge

Although Jo did not know it, her lateness and decision to stand Craig up were partly inspired by revenge. In hurting him, she could feel as if she was getting her own back on all those men who had hurt her.

A belief in couple relationships

Given Jo's history you might be forgiven for wondering if she really does have a belief that couple relationships can work. But Jo has stuck at two committed relationships – the second lasting five years. In both cases, the men broke the commitment by having affairs. Jo also decided to see Craig when she might have decided to give up on men altogether. She obviously has some willingness to try to make a partnership work.

A desire to sustain commitment

Jo seems to have a willingness to try her hardest to keep a shaky relationship on track. It is true that she left Derek when he admitted the affair, but in both cases with her previous boyfriends she stayed in the relationship for a period of time once the affairs had begun. Partners of people who have affairs often 'know' about the affairs, but block the knowledge psychologically so that the partnership can be maintained. It seems as if this may have happened to Jo. It is possible that she learnt this from her mother who stuck by her father although he repeatedly broke his promises about giving up gambling. From the outside, it is tempting to judge this kind of behaviour, seeing it as 'doormat' behaviour in which Jo and her mother tolerate things that should not be tolerated. But it is also possible to see this as a blueprint for determination in a relationship, and a desire to make things work, even in adversity. This could be a useful quality for Jo.

Remnants of grief

Jo has lost two men she loved and cared about. She is still mourning their loss and it is these feelings that may be preventing her from enjoying the idea of going out with Craig. Sadness and loss can create a barrier between two people that prevents the natural flow of communication even when this is desired. Sometimes guilt at making a new relationship after a previous one has ended can also cause difficulties. This can happen even when the relationship has ended acrimoniously, as in Jo's case.

What is in your backpack?

Now it is your chance to explore what you may be carrying in your emotional backpack from previous relationships. Try the following exercise to help you make sense of what you bring to new relationships.

Step One

Think back to past relationships that you have been involved in. You can go back as far as you like. Include school romances or first boyfriends or girlfriends. Use the following table to note what you may have learnt from these relationships. Avoid concentrating only on the negative. Look for constructive ideas and beliefs, even in relationships that have not gone well. If you have not had many relationships, use friends' and relatives' partnerships to help you think about what you carry when you first approach relationships.

I am carrying:	I got this from:	It is important to me because:
(*In this column list all the items you think you are carrying in your backpack. For instance, you might decide you are carrying tolerance, or a sense of humour, or a quick temper. Try to list as many qualities as you can.*)	(*In this column list where you think the corresponding quality came from. For instance, you might feel you learnt how to be tolerant in a relationship with a partner who had children that you looked after.*)	(*In this column list why this quality is important to you. For instance, you may recognise that tolerance has helped you to be patient and under-standing in other relationships.*)

Step Two

Now is the time to do a little sorting. Now that you have unpacked your luggage, imagine all the issues you have written about in the columns above, laid out on your bed after your journey. You know you must wash and repair some, throw some away and keep others. Look at what you have written in your table and try to decide if the qualities you have described come into one of three categories – keep, work on or ditch. Work your way down the columns and mark each one with a K (keep), a W (work on) or a D (ditch) according to what you think you would like to do. As you do this try to think about why some things are important and why you need to keep them. For example, you may be tempted to throw away a certain natural instinct to be wary of new relationships, telling yourself you ought to be more spontaneous. But sometimes the ability to stand back and take stock of your feelings early in a relationship can prevent you from diving into an unsuitable partnership.

Step Three

Now that you have marked your columns and thought about what you really need, have a think about what may need working on. For instance, if you are the kind of person who is very enthusiastic about new relationships but soon feels bored, it is important to try and figure out why this happens. You may not want to jettison the enthusiasm because this is an enjoyable side of new relation-ships, but you would like to be less of a 'love junkie' jumping from one relationship to another. If it would help, talk to a friend or relative about the issue, or try writing or taping your ideas about why this is happening. It is surprising how much help this can be because as you put your thoughts into words your feelings and reasoning can often become clearer. If you do decide to talk to someone else, pick your confidant with care. Choose someone you can trust and who can be honest, but not rude, as you share your concern. Their most important attribute must be to listen, so avoid your chatty mates!

Step Four

Now you are at the 'repacking' phase. As you think about the attitudes and emotions you want to put back in your backpack, try to imagine what influence they might have in a new relationship. You may want to repack your ability to talk to anyone, but could your new partner feel jealous if you do this at every club and party you attend. This is not to say you should not retain this attribute, just that you need to think how you will use it, in the same way that a mountain climber, with limited space in his backpack, thinks hard about whether his fleece will serve him as well in the foothills as on the mountain tops. The ability to adapt your approaches to relationships and to work with a partner, rather than against them, will be the single most important item you hold, so it is vital that you consider whether your attitudes are light and flexible, or heavy and set in stone.

Now you have had the chance to consider what might be in your personal relationship backpack, the next section will deal with common relationship problems. Each one will be followed by a case study to help you understand the way in which this difficulty can affect couples and individuals.

Common relationship problems that come from the unknown contents of emotional backpacks

Arguments

Most couples argue at some time. In fact, if you never argue it may be a sign that you have lost all interest in the relationship. An argument (but not a violent row, which is a different issue altogether) can often tell you a great deal about what is going on in a relationship. For instance, have you ever noticed that you (or friends and family) tend to argue about the same things over and over again? This is a common pattern, and it usually begins with a minor squabble over whose turn it is to do the washing-up and ends up in World War III! This is because couples have a tendency to squash angry feelings – most of us are brought up to be polite and not show anger – and then they vent all the small annoyances at once! Or it may indicate something more serious, such as a lack of trust or anxiety about some external issue, such as work or children.

CASE STUDY

Harry and Dora had been married for fifteen years, but felt they often argued over stupid things. Harry had been brought up to be a tidy person, while Dora was much more relaxed about keeping things neat. Harry nagged Dora about her profligate ways with newspapers, but it had little effect. Dora, on the other hand, found the constant tidying and sorting extremely irritating. They had different attitudes tucked away in their backpacks – Harry had the same approach as his grandmother who had brought him up with a straightforward axiom: 'Keep things tidy and life will be simple.' Dora had a set of attitudes gained from living with a friend in a flat during the 1960s when she had a series of liberal experiences with many men. Her attitude could be summed up as, 'Gather ye rosebuds while ye may'! Although they were very different in their feelings about tidiness, they had a great deal else in common, and so the rows about untidiness were annoying rather than a huge disturbance.

For Harry and Dora, arguments were part of the price they paid to stay with each other because they had such different attitudes to one part of their life together.

General communication problems

As a counsellor, I often meet couples who carry completely different approaches to communication in their personal backpacks. (You will also have read more about communication issues earlier in this book.) It is true that men and women tend to deal with communication in a different way. Men often announce their intentions without communicating their thinking process, whereas women tend to discuss their thinking at each stage of a decision. This can mean that neither partner fully understands what their partner is trying to communicate. This process is complicated when you are carrying particular messages about communication in your emotional backpack.

CASE STUDY

Tina and Max had lived together for just over three years when they ran into problems talking about starting a family. Tina was keen to have a baby, but could not understand why Max found it so hard to discuss the issue. When Tina asked him to explain how he felt, Max said things like, 'It's really up to you,' or 'I don't mind – it's your body after all.' Tina eventually exploded, demanding that Max make some sort of statement about where he stood. As they talked it emerged that Max had been engaged some years before and his fiancée had become pregnant. Max had wanted the child, and tried to convince his partner, Susan, to have the baby, even though they were quite young. Susan hardly engaged with the process of deciding what to do, but returned home one evening to announce that she had had an abortion. Max and Susan did not survive this upset to their relationship, and parted soon afterwards. Max had ever afterwards carried (in his emotional backpack) a feeling of rejection and hurt. He shielded his desire to be a father from Tina as he feared that if he seemed too interested or excited, he would trespass on some hidden womanly 'right to choose'. It made little difference that Tina was keen to be a parent – the scar of the episode with Susan remained. Tina, on the other hand, was used to men speaking their mind. Her father and brother were both well able to say what they felt and believed (sometimes too noisily for Tina's mother's comfort) and so she found Max's approach puzzling. She carried an item in her backpack that said something like, 'Men can talk about what they want.' This assumption actually prevented her from being more sensitive to Max's silence.

Sexual concerns

Of all the issues we carry about in our personal backpacks, sex and sexuality seem to generate the most complex and muddled thinking of all. This is perhaps understandable. A sexual relationship is the most intimate relationship of all, and demands the best that you can come up with in negotiating and communication skills. In modern society, we have grown up with many different attitudes to sex – from 'anything goes' to the guidance of religious and cultural practices that each of us may, or may not, adhere to. Sex can be the source of many couples' misunderstandings precisely because of their differing upbringing and experience in sexual matters.

CASE STUDY

Angela and Ryan met at a friend's house one summer evening. The circumstances could hardly have been more romantic. Ryan spotted Angela standing on the lawn in the moonlight, picked a rose and walked down to present it to her. Angela was bowled over by Ryan and they almost immediately began a passionate relationship. They began having sex a very short time after meeting, and at first all was well. Then Ryan began to lose his erection when they started making love. Angela was sympathetic, but after some months, demanded that Ryan admit he was seeing someone else. Ryan said he was not, but Angela told Ryan the relationship was over. Ryan was devastated, and found the blow to his self-esteem very hard to take.

Although neither Angela nor Ryan had time to discover it, they both had sexual messages in their backpacks that collided when they met. Angela had a belief that 'real men are like James Bond – always ready for sex'. Ryan's romantic approach, and the passionate start to their relationship, made her feel that she had indeed found the 'real man' of her dreams. When Ryan began to lose his erection, her fantasies came crashing down. Unable to abandon her dreams, she abandoned Ryan instead. This can often happen if a dream is very strong. It may mean that Angela will never find her ideal man because no man will ever measure up to her unspoken expectations. Ryan also had a powerful message in his backpack. He put women on a pedestal – nothing was too good for them and they should be treated like goddesses. He had imbibed this from his father who had always treated his mother like a saint in human form. Unfortunately, this attitude can carry the seeds of its own destruction because it tends to place the believer under a great strain to see the partner as perfect, avoiding the 'feet of clay' that all of us have. In fact, both Angela and Ryan were searching for a fantasy and may have been doomed to failure once real life broke through.

Work/life balance

This is the issue that many modern couples describe as difficult to negotiate. In many couples both partners work and this can cause differing attitudes, tucked away in emotional backpacks, to crash into one another.

CASE STUDY

Lois and Ivan married when both of them were starting out in their careers – Ivan as a lawyer and Lois in teaching. They had busy lives with long working hours, but reasoned that this would be OK as they were building up their careers to a point when they could relax a little. When Lois, now in her mid-thirties, had reached deputy head at the comprehensive where she worked, she began to feel she wanted a child. Ivan had a good practice and also worked very hard, but was not averse to starting a family and so they began trying for a baby when Lois was thirty-six. Fortunately, Lois became pregnant within six months, and they were both delighted. But then things between them began to deteriorate. Lois felt tired and expected Ivan to take on more of the domestic tasks. Ivan felt he ought to, but also felt exhausted from working. They argued over who should cook the evening meal and Lois accused Ivan of being insensitive and cold. Ivan began to put off going home, while Lois felt miserable and angry. When Lois began her maternity leave, she realised that they could not go on as they were and asked Ivan to talk to her about what was happening. To her surprise, Ivan began to cry and explained he felt he had to 'come up with the goods' now that Lois was pregnant, but felt worried about whether this was possible. Ivan had come from a family where money was always tight, despite the best efforts of his parents. A great many sacrifices had been made to allow Ivan to go to university, and Ivan felt he had to carry on working very hard to keep Lois. Although he could not quite admit it to himself, he had been mixed about becoming a father because he remembered the strain that being a parent had

had on his own parents. Lois had some similar issues about men caring for their partners as her mother had never worked, accepting a traditional role in the care of the family. As they talked about it they began to realise that the uncovered influence of their family life was affecting them as they too became parents.

Second marriages/partnerships

You might be surprised to learn that second marriages are much more likely to end in divorce than first marriages. About six in ten second marriages break down. This seems a strange statistic, as we could speculate that a couple in a second relationship could be older and wiser about how relationships work. But it is not such a mystery when you consider all the stresses and strains on a second partnership – children from one or both relationships to be integrated, financial problems because of payments being made to an ex-wife or husband and the psychological implications of coming out of a stressful relationship and building a new one.

CASE STUDY

Marcus and Kerry met after both had been divorced a year. Kerry had three children, two sons and a daughter, who lived with her. Marcus had one son, who lived with his mother. At first, both were anxious about dating again. Their previous marriages had ended with a great deal of acrimony, especially for Kerry, because of financial difficulties. At the time of seeing Marcus she was still heavily in debt. Marcus saw his son most weekends, but often felt unhappy about missing the everyday moments of being with him. They shared their mutual nervousness, and this became a bond for them as they felt that other friends in similar situations had often raced into new relationships, with disastrous results. After ten months of dating, Marcus suggested that they move in together. Kerry agreed and they found a rented house nearby. Kerry hoped that her children would accept Marcus, which they did reasonably well. However, some problems developed over sharing the paying of bills and creating bank accounts. Kerry felt she could not let Marcus know about her accounts, and often hid the real amount of money she had in the bank. Marcus found this very frustrating. He reasoned that he trusted Kerry, so why did she not trust him? A difficulty also developed over his behaviour towards Kerry's children. Kerry felt he was less tolerant with her daughter than with her sons. Kerry had observed that her daughter was often told off for doing something her sons got away with.

The problems that Kerry and Marcus encountered had to do with experiences that had found their way into their emotional backpacks from their marriages. Kerry's husband, Louis, had been a real spendthrift and often landed them in debt. This experience had made her very wary of letting anyone else near her precious savings and caused her to block out Marcus's attempts to share their financial concerns. Marcus missed his son very much and made up for this by treating Kerry's sons differently to her daughter. He behaved towards them as if they were his own son, rather than seeing the need for fairness.

Essential items in your emotional backpack

What you carry into your future relationships can have a profound effect on the success of those relationships. If you carry out the exercise above you can help yourself to make sense of what you think you need, and what is not needed. Here is a list of some items that can help a relationship to succeed and that you definitely want in an emotional backpack. You could regard these as the torch and first aid kit of your journey through relationship development!

The willingness to develop trust

Trust is probably the key element of most relationships. How you want to trust your partner is up to you. For instance, you may want to trust that although your partner has affairs, they will always come back to you. Or you may want to trust that they will keep their promise never to leave you. Whatever you decide is the perimeter of your trust in a given relationship, it is important that you are at least willing to discuss how to create and build on trust with a partner.

An openness to negotiation

If you begin relationships always believing you are right, or hoping that your potential partner will change according to your desires, you will probably find your relationship is unfulfilling and tense. An openness to negotiate and see things from your partner's point of view occasionally can create a relationship that is really invigorating and stress-free. This does not mean you have to be a doormat, always accepting your partner's point of view. It is important that you can put your own view, with vigour if needed, but that you can also try to understand what your partner is asking for.

An ability to adapt

In the story of Cinderella and Prince Charming the whole series of events takes place before they fall in love. Once together, we are not told how their marriage proceeded. For all we know they were divorced within five years, although of course we hear 'they lived happily ever after'. Like this fairy story, it is tempting to imagine that once set up, relationships go on as they begin. It is true that it is important to put down some foundations to a partnership, but the ability to adapt and change in different circumstances is also essential. For example, imagine you get together with a man or a woman who is very wealthy. You may look forward to a lifetime of financial security and plan accordingly. Then they take a terrible tumble on the stock market, and lose almost all their money. Could the relationship survive? The same tests can apply to people who find they have a life threatening illness, have a child who needs full-time care because of a physical or mental disability or have a partner who develops a mental health problem. Not all relationships can survive these concerns, but the ability to make adaptations and seek for new ways of coping with relationship difficulties can help you to feel more secure, and perhaps surprisingly, stable.

A strong sense of self-esteem

Feeling good about yourself is one of the essential prerequisites to making a relationship work well. This does not mean you have to be happy or regard yourself as beautiful at all times – just that it is helpful to feel some degree of self-confidence because it is then easier to allow the relationship to develop in a natural and less constricted manner. If you have strong expectations that the relationship will make you feel better about yourself ('if I could only go out with him or her, everything in my life will fall into place') then you are almost 99 per cent likely to be disappointed. No one person can meet all your needs. It is true that some relationships can be redemptive – that is, they are so supportive to one or both partners that a sense of self-worth blossoms – but this is rarely because one partner is feeding off the confidence of the other. It is usually because they feel supported and cared for and this allows a sense of who they can be to grow. It is not easy to define where self-esteem comes from, but it is usually a mixture of physical, mental, emotional and spiritual health. Again, I am not suggesting you need to be an athlete, ecstatically joyous, or a great philosopher, only that you need to feel relatively comfortable with these aspects of yourself in order to have a relationship that makes you happy.

These essential items in your backpack should mean that you take decisions about the suitability of your love life that create more of the above attributes, rather than deplete them by making decisions that fill your backpack with issues that feel heavy and unhelpful. For example, Olivia was recovering from a messy divorce which had been characterised by arguments and recriminations. Two months after the decree nisi arrived on her doormat, Olivia met Samuel. Samuel pursued Olivia, often arriving at her flat door with bunches of flowers and making dates at expensive restaurants. Olivia was flattered, and wanted to go out with Sam, but held back. She knew in her heart that it was too soon for her to commit to a new relationship, especially one with someone like Samuel who was so demanding. She knew she needed more time to recover from the trauma of the divorce if she was to preserve her self-esteem. Having talked this through with Samuel, he cooled down and called round for coffee occasionally instead. They did eventually go out together, but Olivia felt she was much more in control, and able to handle the prospect of a new relationship.

Feeling weighed down?

Having looked at some of the 'must haves' on your love journey, here are some attitudes within relationships that you can definitely do without. These are the equivalent of carrying a load of wet washing around with you and they contribute nothing towards the future of a partnership.

Blame

As you meet and develop new relationships with others you may find that the tricky issue of fault arises when you are talking about something that has caused a problem. From who forgot to bring their credit card for a meal out to why it is so tough to get on with his parents, couples are great at throwing blame and fault around. But most of the time this is a futile occupation. Think about it this way. If you want someone else to take all the blame for a difficulty, you are really asking to feel guilt-free. This might allow you to occupy the moral high ground, but rarely solves the problem. Eventually you will have to find a way to come down to where your partner is. Added to this is the likelihood that they will be feeling bitter and frustrated and planning how to get their own back on you. Instead of flinging blame around, think about what responsibilities you both have for a given situation. For example, Molly felt really angry with Mike for persistently leaving his dirty crockery in the sink without washing it up. She angrily washed it up, evening after evening, saying nothing to Mike and banging the plates and mugs around, and then flinging herself into the sofa with a big sigh. She could not believe that Mike had not got the message, but he still left the unpleasant surprise every time she came home from work. One evening, after an especially tiring day at work, she exploded at Mike, telling him he was lazy and uncaring. Mike was astounded, and appeared speechless. After a while he said, 'But I didn't think you minded. You do it for me every night. I just thought you were showing me how much you cared.' He had missed all the signals that went along with Molly's anger. In this situation, Molly had blamed Mike for being uncaring and unobservant. But she had responsibilities in the situation that could have prevented the problem escalating in the first place. Her responsibility was to talk to Mike about the washing-up instead of hoping her 'martyr' act would be picked up. Mike had some responsibilities to stop taking Molly for granted. Try to look at new situations with an eye on what possible responsibilities come to the fore. Pre-empting what you might be responsible for can prevent all sorts of difficulties. You may find, for example, that you have a responsibility to remain sober on a wild night out, to say sorry if you have hurt someone's feelings, to protect a friend from another's gossip, and so on.

Making assumptions

If you find yourself making assumptions about your partner you may find that the relationship will soon run into trouble. To be fair, it is easy for this to happen. You may think that you know your partner reasonably well and assume they think or believe something that they do not. This is especially important at the start of a relationship as it is harder to retrieve the situation if you have made long-term assumptions. Tom found this when he started going out with Elaine. Elaine had just broken up with a boyfriend and Tom assumed that she was not looking for a long-term relationship. Tom wanted a fairly light liaison 'just for fun' and assumed this was what Elaine would want too. Seven weeks later Tom told Elaine that he had met someone else and was distressed to find that Elaine broke down in tears and was very upset. Elaine had assumed that Tom was making a deeper commitment, and had begun to fall in love with Tom. Tom might have ameliorated some of this situation if he had explained his intentions at the start, although Elaine still might not have been able to prevent herself falling for him. She could, however, have resigned herself to the situation and avoided some of the consequent pain of losing him.

Fantasising

Every love song you have ever heard is full of the joys (and heartbreaks) of love. Many are also full of fantasies about what it would be like to be with the ideal partner. Unfortunately, although it is natural to fantasise a little about a prospective partner, this is very different from thinking rationally about what kind of partner you need. Fantasising can lead to some distinct problems. For instance, if you spot someone on your street whom you like the look of and then spend three months fantasising about their wonderful personality, their properties as a red-hot lover or their desire to support the same football team, only to discover that they are none of these things, you may feel there will never be anyone right for you. This creates an artificially high barrier for both you and a prospective partner to leap over, and probably forms a path to low self-esteem. Repetitive fantasising can cut you off from the real world, leaving you unable to relate to those possible partners you do meet. If you know you do this, it may be that you are scared of facing the world and all the struggles it may take to find a partner you can feel comfortable with. Setting your partner in stone as a beautiful, but unreal, statue on a pedestal is unfair and will lead to a crash as you both face what you really are.

Cynicism

If you have been through some broken relationships in the past, it is easy to feel cynical about a new partnership. Some cynicism is a defence against being hurt again – 'I'll just wait and see if he/she keeps their promise. I bet they don't if they're anything like my last one. All men/women are the same' – and this is understandable. You may feel extremely wary about wearing your heart on your sleeve if the last time you did this it was crushed. The problem with cynicism is that it is like a lens. Looking at every relationship through such a lens can eventually make you feel very bitter and you expect less from every person you meet. It is OK to be hurt after a hurtful break-up – you would not be human if you weren't – but try not to assume that every other man or woman will behave in the same way. Judge people on what they do rather than what you think they will do. This does not mean suspending your instinct or failing to make sensible judgements about whether a relationship is good for you or not, just that you do not need to put every potential partnership in jeopardy because you (or those you cared for) were hurt in the past.

In conclusion

This chapter has looked at the influences that past relationships and/or learning about relationships have had on you. This has taken the form of looking into 'an emotional backpack', allowing you to understand what you are 'carrying' when you approach a new relationship.

Some of the chief problems in relationships have been addressed, and an analysis of essential backpack items has been suggested. You will also have read about those concerns that may weigh you down emotionally and which should be jettisoned. Now you are ready to go on to consider what kind of partner you are looking for.

4

Who is Right For Me? And How Do I Find Them?

In the first three chapters, you concentrated on your learning from previous relationships and also on the influence of your upbringing. You explored what attitudes and beliefs you brought to new relationships, and whether these were reasonable or needed revamping. This chapter is in two parts. The first part is aimed at helping you to think about the kind of partner you are looking for. The second will offer some ideas on finding that partner.

Part One

Magnet relationships

What kind of partner do you usually find you are drawn to? Most people do have a pattern, although they may not always recognise what it is. Sometimes the attraction to others follows a repeating relationship path. For instance, Vivien found herself drawn to older men who were often just coming out of a relationship or who seemed able to take her out and give her treats. She often found that the relationships started very well, but began to fizzle

71

out when the men asked for more commitment from her. Her longest relationship had lasted a year, and she had had many more of only a few weeks or months. Vivien felt dissatisfied with this situation, but could not prevent herself from being attracted to this kind of man.

Vivien was magnetically attracted to older men. That is, she felt pulled towards this kind of man, even though she was unsure if the relationship was exactly what she wanted. Some magnetic attractions work out very well. The couple are mutually attracted, and discover that this is because they have a great deal in common. Others are less successful, with partners caught in an attraction that seems to be against their deeper wishes. Often they are a triumph of hope over experience – the relationship starts out well, with one or both partners telling themselves 'this time it will all be different'. Then things begin to go wrong, or the relationship does not live up to the image that the participants have.

To discover if you are drawn to a particular kind of partner, here is a questionnaire for you to fill in. Tick the box that best describes your interest in others. For instance, if you are often attracted to tall men, tick the 'often' box. Some of your answers will depend on different circumstances, but try to answer according to your immediate response to the questions.

Attraction rating	Always	Often	Sometimes	Occasionally	Never
Physical attributes					
Tall men					
Tall women					
Short men					
Short women					
Slim					
Plump					
Large					

Attraction rating	Always	Often	Sometimes	Occasionally	Never
Muscular					
Average					
Blonde					
Brunette					
Redhead					
Brown eyes					
Blue eyes					
Green eyes					
Other eye colour					
Long hair					
Short hair					
Age					
16–24					
25–34					
35–44					
45–54					
55–64					
65–74					
75–84					
An age difference of no more than five years either way					
Should be older than me					
Should be younger than me					

Attraction rating	Always	Often	Sometimes	Occasionally	Never
Should be the same age as me, give or take a year or two					
Personality and character					
Outgoing and lively					
Quiet and reserved					
Talkative					
A good listener					
Sociable					
Happy with their own company					
Similar interests to me					
Different interests to me					
Able to show feelings					
Good at making decisions					
Authoritative					
Good at negotiating					

Attraction rating	Always	Often	Sometimes	Occasionally	Never
Personal circumstances					
Educated to degree level					
Educated to GCSE level					
Financially well off					
Financially moderately well off					
Financial circumstances unimportant					
Has been married/in a long-term relationship before					
Has never had a long-term relationship before					
Has children from a previous partnership					
Does not have children from a previous relationship					
Is working					
Is not working					
Owns home					

Attraction rating	Always	Often	Sometimes	Occasionally	Never
Home owner-ship not important					
Student					
Hobbies and interests					
Enjoys sport					
Enjoys con-temporary music					
Enjoys classical music					
Enjoys reading					
Enjoys dancing (of different types)					
Enjoys eating out					
Enjoys shop-ping					
Enjoys film and/or TV					
Enjoys a shared specialist inter-est (e.g. train-spotting, bird watching, painting etc)					
Religious and spiritual beliefs					
Shares same religious and spiritual beliefs					

Attraction rating	Always	Often	Sometimes	Occasionally	Never
Has an interest in spirituality but could be of a different faith or none					
Does not share spiritual beliefs at all					
Ethnicity					
Shares the same ethnic background					
Does not share same ethnic background, but has sympathy with it					
Does not share same ethnic background and knows little about it					
Sexuality					
Is heterosexual					
Is homosexual					
Is bisexual					
Wants frequent sex					
Wants moderate amount of sex					
Enjoys sexual experimentation					

Attraction rating	Always	Often	Sometimes	Occasionally	Never
Is sexually conservative					
Is a virgin					
Has had many sexual partners					
Has had a few sexual partners					

Now that you have filled in the questionnaire, take a look back at the categories and note what you have ticked. For some questions you will have been able to make a quick decision. For others, it may have taken you longer. It would have been natural if you had felt that your partners fitted several of the categories, but you will probably now be able to see a pattern to the kind of partner you have most often been drawn to. Now write out on a separate piece of paper the picture you have gained from the questionnaire. The following is an example to help you.

Karen's list
Karen filled out the questionnaire and when she wrote down what she found attractive and/or magnetic, she came up with this:

Physical attributes
Tall men who could be plump or average build. Usually blonde with blue eyes and short hair.

Age
Usually 35–44 (Karen is 36), with an age difference of no more than five years either way, but preferred older.

Personality and character
Outgoing and lively, often talkative. Several have had different interests to Karen and can show feelings. Less good at making decisions.

Personal circumstances

Usually educated to GCSE or O level standard and in full-time work. Financially, moderately well off with their own home. Often has only had a couple of committed relationships, although this has not often been seen as very important.

Hobbies and interests

Enjoys music and dancing (Karen often goes to a local line-dancing club). Some have been interested in reading, films or other interests shared with Karen.

Religious and spiritual beliefs

Karen has no formal religious belief and has never been attracted to a man who has an expressed interest in religion or spirituality.

Ethnicity

Karen has usually been with men of the same ethnic background as her.

Sexuality

Karen is attracted to men who are heterosexual and enjoy a moderate amount of sexual activity. She has met men who have had a few previous sexual partners, but never been out with a man who has never had a previous sexual partner.

Karen was surprised to find that she did have a pattern. Looking back over the previous three years, she had been out with men who more or less fitted the pattern that she came up with when she wrote out the findings. One or two of her dates had been transitory – just going out for a drink – while others had lasted a month or two. None had led to a serious commitment, although Karen was certainly open to finding a man to make a commitment to.

Once you have undertaken this exercise, go back to the list. Use a different colour pen or pencil and tick each box again. This time, mark the kind of attribute you would want a potential partner to have, but have not explored. For instance, you might decide that although you always seem to have had relationships or dates with brunettes, you would like to go out with a redhead. Allow yourself to consider attributes and abilities that you might otherwise have overlooked. For example, Karen noted that she normally found herself with men who were talkative and outgoing, but realised that this meant she often overlooked the quieter and more reserved man. She felt she did this because she thought this kind of man might be 'boring', but she remembered many occasions when a loud partner had made her feel she would rather be with a man who was quieter and a better listener. Repeat your list and then think through why you have not found yourself in a relationship with the kind of person who has emerged from your second list.

For instance, Karen realised that she was drawn to men who were quite authoritative because she found making decisions hard. She had been out with men who were more considerate, but often found herself vacillating about decisions because her partner did not say what he wanted. Karen realised that she often went out with men who were a little callous – uncaring about her personal desires – and that this happened because she found it hard to admit, even to herself, that she had specific wants and needs.

What are your standards?

Now that you have two lists – one of those partners you are often drawn to and another of those that you have met less – you will need to reflect on what standards you have in relationships. This is a bit of a taboo subject. One of the most common romantic dreams is that couples meet and accept each other as they are. But all of us do have standards – often unspoken or unacknowledged. We might feel we could never date a short man or a redheaded woman, regardless of their character. Or the thought of going out with someone who did not enjoy football or going to the cinema could be a complete 'no-no'. Other standards might be connected to ethnicity or religious beliefs. It is OK to have these standards, but beware of blocking out on a whim partners who could be just right. For instance, Kim decided that she could never date a bald man, and so screened out all bald men she met, even though several could have been good for her to get to know. Allow yourself to expand a little beyond your usual standards, although you may still want to keep one or two, such as never going out with someone who eats with their mouth open or who fails to pay their way on a date.

Use your lists to help you identify what your secret standards might be. Mark with an asterisk all the boxes that might relate to one of your 'standards'. Now go back to the start and question yourself about why you have chosen the 'standards' you have. Aim to eliminate as many as possible, ending up with the ones you know are vital to you. For example, John removed a 'standard' that he realised was related to his mother, and her attitudes rather than his, about only going out with women who were younger than him. John's mother had once expressed distaste when he had brought a woman home who was a couple of years older than him. John had unconsciously received the idea that dating such women was 'wrong', and had consequently avoided older women for years.

The aim of looking back at your lists in this way is to help you develop a confidence about finding a partner who suits you, but also to help you see that you do not always have to stick in a 'relationship rut', with the same kinds of partners who you may, or may not, feel are right for you.

Different styles of relationships

All relationships are unique. No two can be said to be exactly the same. But there are relationship styles that many couples fit into, even if their relationship fit is not exactly the same. Here are some common styles of relationships. As you read them, ask yourself what kind of relationships you have previously been in and what style you would like to have in the future.

The protection club

This kind of relationship is more common than you might imagine. Usually, one partner appears to protect the other – often the man the woman – offering a barrier against the difficulties of the world outside. To onlookers, it may appear that the one who is protected is weaker and in need of looking after. Sometimes the relationship is characterised by the man telling the woman that she does not need to work or that she should commit herself to the home. But this picture of one person protecting the other hides another story. The partner who appears stronger may well have chosen the seemingly weaker precisely because they need to feel that they are strong and capable, and a partner who seems to need their care can help to provide this. It is interesting to note that often the couple unconsciously agree to play these roles. If one partner dies, the other will suddenly start to do things for themselves, proving that they had hidden capabilities that were suppressed for the sake of the relationship. In many ways, both partners protect each other, allowing the relationship to seem like a partnership between stronger and weaker individuals.

The quarrelsomes

Most couples argue, but the quarrelsome couple seem to make an art form from bickering! This kind of arguing can be extremely wearing, but some couples seem to conduct their relationship at this level all the time. They may spend their time needling each other and falling out over trivial matters, but they still stay together. Often this kind of relationship is one where both partners are afraid of expressing their often deep feelings for one another, and use the rows to cover their anxiety about appearing vulnerable. A variation on this theme is the use of humour. One or both of the partners may use jokes (sometimes at the other's expense) to cover other emotions. Sometimes this kind of arrangement occurs because one or other of the partners has been hurt in a previous relationship. If they have exposed their feelings for another, and had these trampled on, they may fear that this could happen again and so disguise their emotions by arguing with or joking about a partner.

The marriage of equals

This is probably the relationship that many of us aspire to. A matched partnership where similar interests are shared. Often this kind of couple share a passion for something important in their lives such as working in a shared business or similar careers. This couple often seem very happy, but they can encounter problems if anything undermines their togetherness. For instance, if their shared business begins to fail they may feel that their relationship is also in trouble.

The romantics

In this relationship, both partners seem wrapped up in each other to such an extent that they seem to shut out the rest of the world. Friends and relations may feel excluded by the closeness of the partnership, or worry that one day real life will intervene, causing the relationship to fail. This phase of a relationship often occurs in the early months of a couple getting together, and although it can last for some while, is often replaced by a more pragmatic approach to life. For those couples who are still besotted with each other after years together, the romance may serve a purpose in acting like a glue that keeps them together. To insist that they stop looking at each other, and consequently the world, through rose-coloured glasses, would be to ruin the relationship. They may be quite naïve, but their romantic lifestyle can act as an effective cushion against the slings and arrows of everyday life.

The pragmatics

This couple have an emotional bond that is made up of a sensible approach to life. They are completely opposite to the romantics and may seem to be motivated only by good sense and logic. They often have a very organised lifestyle, sometimes envied by friends who despair of ever having such order in their lives. Other people may more unkindly brand them 'control freaks' but their brand of organisation can make them feel as if they are in control of life. They are the sort of people who give each other household items for birthdays and Christmas rather than gold necklaces, but can often be very happy with this arrangement. They are unlikely to be outwardly demonstrative, but often harbour a private warmth that might surprise those who know them.

Opposites attract

In this partnership the couple seem to have very little in common. One may be an outgoing party animal while the other is a home lover. On the surface it may appear that they have nothing to offer each other, but this kind of complementary relationship can often work because each partner makes up for what the other lacks. The quieter partner can steady the excesses of the louder one, and the more outgoing partner can encourage the shyer one to be more sociable. This is why some improbable partnerships can stand the test of time. This kind of relationship can be thrown off track if one partner begins to change or if they gradually become more and more polarised, so that they exist at opposite ends of the scale rather than comfortably apart.

Two on a mission

Some couples are brought together by a particular cause. I am not necessarily describing the couple who both believe passionately in organic farming or saving the rainforests, although many couples find that this kind of shared ethos is part of the concrete of their relationship. By 'cause' I mean any shared ideology that causes the partners to feel a close bond and direction. For instance, a couple might want to be parents, with fixed ideas about what a family will mean to them, or they may want to work together to pursue a dream, such as sailing around the world. One of the difficulties with 'mission' relationships is that they may go very well until the mission is finished. The couple who feel very close until the family they both wanted leave home, or those who achieve their dream, may find that they have been so focussed on the 'mission' that they have forgotten to discover who their partner is and what their specific needs are. Some 'mission couples' simply go on to replace a finished project with another. This kind of relationship can work, but it probably requires both partners to consider what else they want from the relationship in addition to the mission they may have embarked on.

There are variations on all these themes which may have occurred to you as you have been reading this section. You may even have felt that you fit into a particular section, or that one of the relationship styles seems more attractive than the others. You could find it helpful to write some notes of your own, describing the different kinds of relationships you think you may have encountered. Notice if there are repeating patterns, and what this might tell you about your particular choices in relationships. You may find you welcome some styles, but have felt uncomfortable with others. Use your notes and the answers to the previous questionnaires to help you reflect on what you want from a relationship. Thinking about your personal style and preferences can really help you as you move into the next part of this chapter which is concerned with finding a partner.

Part Two

Looking for Mr or Ms Right

You could be forgiven for thinking that finding someone to build a relationship with is a matter of luck. One day you will walk down the street and bump into the man or woman of your dreams. To some extent, there is some truth in this. Many couples describe how they met as 'accidental' rather than carefully planned. But if you want to find a partner, and are perhaps reading this book because you have not had much success in this area, then an understanding of what might make a positive contribution could really help you to develop new ways of meeting potential partners.

If you want to find a partner, some foundations need to be laid before you begin to look seriously. Earlier in the book you will have explored some of the psychological and emotional issues that form part of this set of foundations but there are some other, more practical, issues you will also need to address.

- **Where are you looking?**

  It is not unusual to find that people looking for partners keep looking in the same places! They may go to the same club or pub Saturday night after Saturday night, meeting the same people, but wondering why they are never finding the right person. This is rather like going to a library every week for ten years, borrowing all the books, and then wondering why your reading is so boring! Visiting the same venue month after month will mean that you are likely to meet the same people. Of course, it can be fun to meet up with the same group of friends at weekends. But it may actually hold you back from looking in other areas for a partner who would suit you.

- **Why are you looking?**

  This might seem a rather strange question – after all, you might want to tell me 'because I want a partner, stupid!' But people seek partners for various reasons. You might have just split up with a partner and be looking for someone to have fun with; you might be searching for the love of your life or be looking because your best mate thinks it is a good idea for you to go out with someone. Different venues will suit different reasons. For instance, you might visit a nightclub if you are looking for a short-lived romance or a dating agency if you are looking for a long-term partner.

- **How are you looking?**

  Are you sitting quietly in the corner at the pub hoping that the man or woman you fancy will finally notice you? Or are you racing around at the dance, dancing with as many people as you can? The approach you take to searching is important. It could be that you need to be much more pro-active than you have been, but in a focussed way rather than going off like a scatter gun. You might also be behaving in a certain way because of your age and maturity. Teenagers looking for partners behave very differently to the middle-aged, as you have no doubt noticed! The influence of the group you mix with can be crucial. Their influence on what you expect and how you make relationships can make all the difference to finding a partner because every group has unwritten rules about how you should approach a potential partner. This is especially true if you like the look of someone outside your particular group. You only have to read Shakespeare's 'Romeo and Juliet' to have evidence of this. If you feel you have had little luck where you are, you may have to break the mould in order to find the special person you are looking for.

- *When are you looking?*
  I am not so much thinking of time of day (although this might be important in some ways) but more of what you are bringing to a particular situation. For instance, if you have just suffered a broken heart you will feel very differently to someone who is just starting out on dating for the first time. Your broken heart could cause you to want to take revenge on your next partner, perhaps by not trusting them or by hurting them in the same way that you were hurt. Alternatively, you might be looking for a partner to heal the pain you have been through. If you are just starting, you might approach the whole situation very fearfully or with great excitement. So the 'when' I am thinking of has more to do with the stage in your life and experience at which you are seeking a partner.

Once you have thought about these different areas of approach, you are ready to think about more tangible ways of meeting the person of your dreams.

Looking around

There are many ways of looking for a partner. Some are more popular than others. How you undertake your search is a matter of personal taste, but I would suggest that you spread your net more widely than you have done in the past. Exploring novel ways of meeting others can help to widen your search, allowing you to get away from the repeating circle of disappointment of your current search area.

Clubs and pubs

These can be fun places to meet new people, especially if you enjoy dancing and a lively social atmosphere. They also have some drawbacks in that they are frequently noisy, preventing conversation. You may have to accept that this way of meeting could be a good springboard, but is not conducive to really getting to know someone well. Added to the noise is the complication of alcohol consumption, which can make someone you would normally avoid suddenly seem very attractive! If you do arrange a date, make sure you subsequently meet them somewhere where there are plenty of other people – a café or restaurant is ideal. (There is more on safe dating in the next chapter.)

'Lonely Hearts' columns

Lots of people shy away from these columns, but they can be worth a try if you feel you want to meet people from a wider social circle. Most papers and magazines that run these also print a form for you to fill in or provide a phone service where you call to leave details. In most cases, you will be given a 'mail box' from which replies are forwarded for you to deal with, or a telephone message box where you can listen to respondents' messages. You can print a jokey, or more serious, message according to your tastes, but beware of describing yourself as a very different person to the one you really are. You might attract the wrong kind of person, or make a first date very uncomfortable. Again, follow the safe dating procedure in the next chapter.

Dating and introduction agencies

These are many and varied, and have different kinds of approaches to the same basic premise – that they will act on your behalf to try and find you a partner with similar interests in your locality (or further away if you request this). Some are national, and have contacts all over the UK. Some are very local, promising to deal within a certain area. Others can act on your behalf in foreign countries. All dating and introduction agencies should be treated with caution because of one important fact – they take money from you! Before you part with any cash, be absolutely clear about what they are promising and ask to see any literature about previous success. If possible, ask to speak to a client who has used the service. If you do not get the promised introductions or they are completely unsuitable, complain and ask for a refund. If you do not receive a refund, contact your local Trading Standards department who will be able to help you regain your costs if the firm has reneged on the deal. Remember that this kind of introduction is not an exact science. The person who looks ideal on paper could be completely wrong in reality. Do not forget to follow safe dating procedures.

Supper groups

This is a new way of meeting friends (who might turn into dates). The idea is that the agency books a restaurant, or similar venue, and invites ten to twelve people on its list to attend a supper together. You will need to register with the agency in the same way as with an introduction agency, but the manner of meeting is less 'set up', allowing you to talk to those around the table in a natural way. It can also mean that if you do not want to take things further with anyone at the supper, you can slip away without going through the embarrassing 'goodbye' to a person you know you do not wish to meet in the future. These kinds of groups are mushrooming around the country, so look in your local paper or Yellow Pages for a group close to you.

Event groups

These operate in a similar way to supper groups in that they arrange events which you can, for a payment, have access to. Usually the events are circulated to members and take part in many different parts of the UK. Events can include parties at festival times, weekends in country hotels, sports meetings, barbecues and so on. These kinds of groups can be great if you are on your own in a new part of the country and want to get to know others of a similar mind to yourself. You will usually join a mailing list and receive a regular bulletin to help you keep in touch with what is going on. The emphasis is on natural meetings rather than set up dates with just one person. Check out national and local media for information on these groups.

Divorced and separated clubs

Many towns and cities now have these groups who meet regularly to support people who have been divorced or separated. Although they may not have the deliberate aim of bringing people together, in reality they often do. If you have both gone through the same problem, it can create a bond that you find very helpful and this can lead to attraction and love. Look in your local Yellow Pages for these groups.

Other ideas for meeting potential dates

Although all the above ideas are tried and tested, there are some less well-known ways of meeting a partner. Why not try some of these?

Bookstores

Lots of bookshops now offer coffee bars alongside their book sales. You might bump into someone reading a book you have loved, or sit at a table with someone who chats about a book they really like. The good thing about this is that you can legitimately share a table and start a conversation if you would like to.

Interest and hobby groups

No, you don't have to have an anorak to join an interest group! If you have any hobby that you would like to develop, especially one that is open to men and women, try joining your local group. If you enjoy sport, then this kind of group can be very useful – even at a 'beginner' standard. For instance, you might consider a ramblers' group, learn salsa dancing, play badminton, join a 'cycling for fun' group or just play darts at your local. All of these can help you to meet new people and widen your circle of friends.

Volunteering

Working with others on a charitable exercise can bring you into contact with people who share your concerns and create an immediate bond of interest. Some volunteering is physical – rebuilding dry stone walling or clearing out old canals – while in other cases you might be writing letters of support or creating posters for a rally. Whatever you feel interested in supporting, there is almost certainly a group of people in your area you could meet up with.

Further education

Taking a course in something you would like to know more about can be a good way to meet others with similar interests. For instance, you might choose to learn a new language, or to get to grips with the basics of mechanics or cookery. A good tip here is to brave a class that is normally seen as being a man's or woman's topic. If you are a woman, consider woodwork; if a man, think about flower arranging. If this seems a bit too much, stick to neutral things like creative writing or painting.

Group holidays

Many travel firms now run holidays for single people who share a holiday venue as a group. For instance, you might enjoy a walking holiday in Greece or a wine-tasting weekend in France with a group of people who are also on their own. Ask at your local travel agent for information on groups who run this kind of holiday.

E-mail and chat rooms

If you are on-line you may have already discovered that there are thousands of Internet chat rooms where you can enter discussions on everything under the sun. There are also a variety of on-line dating agencies, who operate in a very similar way to the usual kind of dating agency in that they take your details and, for a fee, will link you to the person who fits your preferences. Chat rooms involve you entering a group conversation, and then, if you feel confident, talking privately to just one person. There are some dangers in this approach because the person you are e-mailing may not be what they say they are. They could tell you that they are tall and blonde when in fact they are short and dark. It is easy to be taken in by this kind of communication, so I urge caution if you are communicating in this way. (Read the safety guidelines in the next chapter.) If you are looking for an arranged marriage, there are specialist websites that allow you to enter your details in order to find a partner who might be suitable for you.

Checklist for which method might be good for you

If you are thinking about trying one of these methods for finding a partner, use the following checklist to help you decide which one is best for you.

Style of partnership
Ask yourself what sort of relationship you are looking for. For instance, if you want a casual kind of partnership, a pub or supper club could be right for you. You could have some fun for just one night without feeling you have to make a commitment to seeing the person every week. Alternatively, if you prefer to develop a relationship over a longer period of time, a hobby group could be a good alternative. Dating agencies can also allow you to explore what kind of relationship you are aiming for without making a commitment to everyone you meet.

Financial considerations
Your financial situation can be important in deciding which method you will employ in seeking a partnership. Some dating agencies can be expensive, and may ask for monthly or quarterly fees. (Remember, never commit to giving cash without some assurance that introductions will be forthcoming.) If you have the cash, this may not matter to you, but if you are trying to keep costs down then joining a group or volunteering could be a good option. Think through any hidden costs (such as paying for a meal or staying on an Internet line for hours), and measure these against other methods you have tried in the past.

Social setting

Are you the kind of person who gets on well with a crowd of people? Or do you prefer to be with just a few people? If you are a party animal, some of the supper or event groups might be your cup of tea, while individual dates from a dating agency might be more suitable if you prefer to concentrate on just one person. If you are shy, choosing a further education course as a means to meeting other people can help you because you will have a subject to concentrate on rather than having to make your own conversation.

Personal circumstances

If you have children or dependent adults at home you may find it hard to make an excuse to go out on a date with someone that your family does not know. In this situation, joining an interest group or volunteering could bring you into contact with others in a way that does not necessarily involve telling your relatives until you are ready to do so that you are seeking a partner. If you have a friend who is looking for a partner as well, you might consider joining a dating agency together and asking for foursome dates. This can help deal with the nerves that meeting a new person often causes, and will allow you to feel safer as you get to know your date. This approach could also work well for event-based groups or supper clubs.

Willingness to travel

In geographical terms, some introduction agencies may cast their net widely so if you are not willing to travel miles, it is important to say so at the initial interview. You should also think through whether you could maintain a relationship if your prospective partner is miles away, even if they seem just right for you. Long-distance relationships can succeed, but often need a great deal of work to make sure they meet the needs of both partners.

In conclusion

In this chapter you have been encouraged to think through the types of prospective partner you usually encounter and are attracted to. Then you have been asked to look at what you want from any future relationship and the standards you might have for that relationship and to reflect on the different styles of relationships that you feel could suit you or are similar to those you have had in the past.

The second part of the chapter has suggested a number of approaches to the way in which you might seek a partner.

5

The Dating Game

Have you found yourself on dates that you wish you had never accepted? Or been on a date that ended with you wanting more, while your partner for the evening seemed happy to walk away? If this is you, then this chapter will help you recognise the signs when a potential partner is worth pursuing or when it would be sensible to make a hasty exit!

Conversation – a new skill

Before I get into the intricacies of dating, I want to discuss having a conversation. I can almost hear you asking yourself if I have gone mad! Doesn't everyone know how to have a conversation? Well, maybe not. It may be a new thought to you, but conversations between men and women (and within same-sex relationships) are a comparatively new invention. Theodore Zeldin, the eminent historian of human relationships, has said that although men and women have been talking to one another for millennia, this is the first generation that is actually beginning to have real conversations across the sexes. He suggests that this is because conversations require equality and a willingness to admit that the person you are talking with has something to say. Men and women have given and received instructions from each other, asked for something they needed or exchanged information, but none of these are what we think of as conversations. Now that, in theory at least, women in the affluent West are able to aspire to equality with men, couples can move beyond the stereotypical roles they have occupied to date and begin to discover the 'art of conversation'.

This begs the question as to how to carry out a conversation, especially with someone you hardly know. Many people find that they can start a conversation quite well, but then falter. So here are some ideas to help you have interesting conversations, long before you get to thinking about dating the object of your interest:

- Choose your moment. Finding the right time to talk to someone can be very important. You are unlikely to have a good conversation if you are in a very noisy environment, or where the person you want to chat to is talking to a group of other people. Some nightclubs now have 'chill out' rooms where people can be quiet for a while. If possible, find a fairly quiet spot or try finding a moment to talk when the others in a group are distracted. Pushing your way into a situation, or shouting above loud music, will not make you seem very attractive.

- Avoid preparing a script in your mind about what you will say and when. If you are shy, or unknown to the person you want to strike up a conversation with, a pre-prepared speech will sound false and you may appear almost 'unreal'. If you know you can dry up when talking to strangers, approach the situation by letting them do most of the talking. Not only does this allow you to learn more about them, but most people appreciate someone taking an interest in them. Do not fire questions at them. Instead, say something like 'I was interested to hear you say you work at the local hospital. Which department are you in?' (Once they have told you, you can then go on to ask them to tell you more about their work.) Alternatively, you could ask, 'I was wondering how you know (host's name). How long have you known them?' or even 'What do you think of this painting?'! These are examples of 'open questions or statements' in that they all allow for someone to answer at length, rather than 'closed questions' that can only be answered by yes or no. An example of a 'closed question' is 'Do you think this wine is OK?', to which the answer can only really be yes or no. If you know someone reasonably well, they may answer 'No, I think it is corked.' A person you do not know very well will probably answer 'yes', 'no' or 'I don't know.' This closes a conversation down – you have nowhere to go from yes or no, other than to ask another question and soon you begin to sound like an interrogator rather than a possible friend.

- Be genuine. It is tempting to put on an act to impress someone you like the look of, but most people can see straight through a phoney presentation in a matter of minutes. If you can just be yourself, you will find that you will make a much more positive impact. Be polite and interested, and people will respond to you. It is OK to talk about yourself, but keep your answers brief rather than long and rambling or you run the risk of boring your new friend rigid! For instance, if you meet someone at an art class, comment on the class, what you have enjoyed about the lessons, what artists you like or exhibitions you have been to and ask them about their experiences. Try not to moan or whinge, even if you think the situation merits it. If you do make a complaint, do it with a smile if possible. For example, if you are standing in a bus queue and have been waiting ages, say something like 'I expect five will arrive at once' rather than 'I am sick of standing here waiting for bloody buses that never arrive.' You may *feel* more strongly than making a light remark about the situation, but at a first meeting it is better to err on the positive than the negative as you want to make a good impression. If you really do feel strongly about a particular issue, there will be time to talk about this later when you know each other better, and are deeper into exploring the less obvious parts of your character. The old adage of never talking about religion, politics or sex in polite company has more or less disappeared and in some circles, people talk about little else! But if you want to keep a conversation alive in the early stages of meeting someone new, try not to dive into very deep conversational waters. For example, if you have strong political views it may be OK to mention these, but not to start on a lecture about why the Green Party should win the next election. An exception to this might be when you meet someone at a shared interest or hobby group. For example, if you met at a Green Party group, then this might be a suitable choice of topic.

- Be respectful. It might seem an obvious thing to say, but if you are respectful in a conversation you will get much further than if you treat the person you are talking to as if they are an idiot. This is probably the single most important issue for men and women to take on board. Up until now, there has often been a tendency for men to patronise women – just think of 'the little woman', 'her indoors' or 'she who must be obeyed', all terms used about women when they have dared to voice an opinion. Is it any wonder that women often felt they had to resort to hectoring or demanding when they were not considered as equals in a conversation? It is also important for women to respect men, and not dismiss their ideas as 'typical men' and so on. The key here is that it is OK to disagree with each other as long as you express your opinions without abusing your partner or deciding you are right come what may. Listen to what your friend is saying and, if you disagree, say something like 'I am interested in what you are saying, but I'm not sure if I agree with you. I see it something like this . . .' This might sound a little false, but if you can find your own style then so much the better. Just be sure to honour the other person's opinions alongside your own. (If they begin to express ideas that you just think are plain wrong – such as racial prejudice – then maybe this is not the person for you. Give up and walk away.)
- Listen to what is not said. This might seem a strange concept, but sometimes you may notice gaps in conversation or changes in body language (more on body language later) that you feel are telling you something, but it is hard to know what. For instance, Clive noticed that Geri never discussed her home life. All Clive knew was that she lived with her widowed father. After a few dates, Clive raised the subject by saying 'I've noticed

that whenever the conversation gets round to families, you fall silent. Is there a reason for that?' Geri explained that she found it hard to talk about the death of her mother two years before, and did not want to 'make a fool' of herself with Clive. Clive reassured Geri that she could never do this, and that he was willing to listen to her talk about her bereavement. This deepened their relationship as Geri realised that Clive was sensitive and thoughtful. If there are gaps in conversation, you may leap to fill them. Embarrassing silences can yawn out before you, making everything feel very uncomfortable. But if you can allow some silence you may be repaid in a way that you do not expect. Silence may not indicate that the flow of the conversation has seized up, simply that one or both of you are reflecting on what has already been said. Allowing a little space can often mean that new ideas or thoughts rise to the surface for discussion.

- Have an open mind. If you arrive at a conversation feeling that someone is miles above or below you, the conversation could feel false and tough to stay with. If you think you are more educated, you run the risk of patronising the person you are talking to. If you see them as on a pedestal, you may feel frozen, unable to talk at all. Instead of feeling this way, cultivate an open mind. Listen to what they are saying, or striving to say, and encourage them to discuss what is important to them. Say what you think, and do not be afraid to be honest. As I pointed out earlier, most people can see through an act, and will switch off. If you can be open minded, you will also learn a great deal about your potential partner, giving you valuable information about whether there might be a future in the relationship. Remember that patronising or idealising often spring from the same source – lack of self-esteem. If you have low self-esteem you may find it hard to expose the real you and so put on an act. If you want to take part in good conversations, the truth is that you must sometimes be vulnerable.

- Be careful about using humour. Some people make jokes when they are talking to others and get away with it. Others make jokes, and everybody dreads their opening line – 'Have you heard the one about . . .' Teasing, making personal remarks or laughing at others in the room is a quick way to put people off. Some teasing is OK once you know each other very well, but even then it is something that takes a sure touch to get right. Most humour in these situations is used to create a feeling of 'I am better than you/We are better than them' and so does not lead to a conversation between equals. When meeting another person for the first time, avoid joke telling and doubtful remarks. However, a smile and genuine warmth of character can take you a long way towards developing a conversation that is worth having.

Now that you have read about managing a good conversation, here are some quick 'do's' and 'don'ts' to consider when meeting someone for the first time:

- Do take some time to look smart. There is no need to be dressed in the latest fashion, but clean clothes and an effort to look attractive will help people to feel interested in you. If you are returning to dating after a long gap – perhaps after a divorce, for instance – you may feel anxious about what to wear or how to do your hair. Don't worry – just try to be comfortable rather than a fashion icon.
- Do try to look welcoming. Offer a reasonably firm handshake (not a bone crusher!) and don't forget to smile.
- Don't cover nerves by talking about yourself all evening. Ask the other person about themselves and their interests. (See above.)
- Don't make assumptions about the person you are meeting by just looking at their clothes or personal style. Remember, you can't judge a book by its cover.
- Do be honest about yourself. You may want to sound more impressive than you really are, but if you lie now then you may have a lot of explaining to do later, which could be very embarrassing.

Dating behaviour

How you behave on a first date is extremely important. Although you cannot learn everything about a person on a first date, you can make, or receive, a powerful impression about the person you are dealing with. You may be aware that there is a lot more to learn, and this is right and natural, but you need to think about, and learn how to handle, this phase of dating if you want to find the right partner for you.

A guide to different kinds of dating

It may seem like stating the obvious to say that there are lots of different kinds of dates. Some are more popular than others. You may remember dates you met through a friend with happy memories or recall a dreadful 'blind' date where you felt as if you were paired with a member of the Addams family! Here is a description of the most popular kinds of dates, with some reflections on handling them effectively.

Blind dates

These dates are often arranged between friends who think you would match perfectly with someone they know. The difficulty with this is that their perception of who they think would be great for you is sometimes not yours! If you have seen the film *When Harry met Sally* you may remember the scenes where their friends try to link Harry and Sally up with an assortment of colleagues and acquaintances, most of whom are totally unsuitable, before they finally realise they are meant for each other.

On the following pages is a table of pros and cons regarding blind dates.

For Blind Dates	Against Blind Dates
You can meet people you might otherwise never come into contact with.	You may have to spend time with someone you feel indifferent towards, or positively dislike.
You are 'forced' to meet and talk to a person you might not normally have thought of as interesting, but who turns out to be good company.	You run the risk of feeling bored, frustrated or annoyed for a period of time when you might have wanted to do something more interesting.
If you are in a foursome with another couple (usually the people who have fixed you up) you can share the evening, rather than have to encounter a near stranger alone.	If you really do not like the person, it can sour your relationship with your friend because you may wonder how on earth they thought you would like the person they picked. This can lead you to wonder how they really see you.
Blind dates can often be fun because you can approach them with nothing to lose. If you like the person, this is a bonus.	If you set yourself up to see the date as very important, you may feel very let down if it does not work out.
You can absolve yourself from the responsibility of picking a date.	You may feel slightly out of control and find it difficult to fully enter into the date.
You will have someone (the friend who set you up) to talk to after the date about how things went, which can sometimes help you to decide if you would like to repeat the experience.	You may feel under pressure to discuss all the details of the date with the friend who set you up on the date.
A successful blind date can boost your self-confidence because you can be sure they liked you for who you are.	If the date fails, you may feel anxious about what this says about the impression you make on people when they first meet you.
If you have subsequent dates, you can discuss what drew you together after the first date.	If there are no subsequent dates, you may wonder what went wrong, and have no feedback to help you make a judgement.

For Blind Dates	Against Blind Dates
Friends can sometimes see aspects of your character that you have overlooked, and that do 'gel' with the person they have chosen.	Friends may make a judgement about you that you do not understand, undermining the date before it even 'gets off the blocks'.

You can probably add some of your own ideas about blind dates to the items listed above. Some people do seem to have a taboo about blind dates, regarding them as the kind of thing that only desperate people do! But you might be surprised at how many people start their dating lives as a result of a 'set up' by friends or relatives. Many arranged marriages begin in just this way – with arranged meetings by family members – and are extremely successful. Here are some things you need to take into account when agreeing to a blind date:

- If possible, go with another couple or in a group. This is not only safer (read more on safe dating practice later in this chapter), but also gives you a way of avoiding getting closer if you are not ready or do not like the person you have been teamed with.
- Arrange to meet somewhere in public view, and say what you will wear or look like. This is less important if your date arrives with your friends, but being clear about this will avoid the embarrassment of standing in the rain trying to guess who is your date for the evening.
- Remember, you are probably both as nervous as each other, so give your potential date some slack if they seem less confident than you would like. Be encouraging and friendly and their nerves will probably fade away. This approach will also help to diminish your nerves as well. Thinking about the other person in this way will stop you obsessing about your own feelings.
- If you are going out for a meal, choose food that is simple to eat! This may sound rather stupid, but if you are battling with spaghetti and sauce, or a brittle brandy snap basket that threatens to spray all over the table, you may feel uncomfortable

and embarrassed. I would also advise that you stick to food you know you like, rather than decide to experiment with squid casserole! Your nerves will only be worsened by trying to cover up your distaste, making just the opposite of the good impression you wanted to give.

Dates with people who were previously friends

It is not uncommon for friendship to blossom into attraction, but many people agonise over whether it is wise to turn a successful friendship into a love affair. Some of this anxiety seems to stem from a common romantic myth that goes something like this: 'If you are going to fall in love, it hits you like a bolt from the blue the minute you clap eyes on the person.' This is a very common fantasy, and of course, cuts out the idea that you might make a passionate relationship with someone who 'just grew' on you. But there are benefits to developing an intimate relationship with someone who is/was a friend. Here are just some:

- You know each other very well, and this can give you a head start in creating a close and loving bond.
- You probably already share a mutual circle of friends.
- You do not have to put on an act to impress your potential date because they will already have seen you as a 'real' person.
- You will have developed good communication, which will allow you to talk easily, instead of having to work on this as a new part of your relationship.
- You know you share similar tastes in leisure activities. Where there are differences, you may be more tolerant of these.

In reality, dates with people you have previously regarded as friends are really 'slow burn' relationships. That is, the chances are that you were attracted to each other when you first met, but that this has taken a long time to develop into a close relationship. Perhaps you both spent a long time testing out your real feelings for one another. Or maybe knowing each other as friends confused your true feelings for one another. Whatever the reason, this kind of relationship can be very successful for all the reasons listed above. You may, however, need to take some issues about friends becoming lovers into account. These include:

- Check out that your friend is as happy as you to take the relationship further. For example, Erica and Rob had known each other off and on for five years since they had been at college together. After a party one evening, and somewhat the worse for wear through drinking, they went back to Rob's flat and slept together. In the morning, Rob seemed delighted that this had happened, telling Erica that he had always hoped they would 'take things further'. But Erica was a lot less happy about the situation. She was not at all sure that she wanted to be in an intimate relationship with Rob, and made excuses to leave. As the weeks passed, she stopped phoning Rob and gradually their association faded. Erica and Rob demonstrate the problems involved in stepping up to a different level with a friend without talking or thinking through the consequences. Erica and Rob both lost not only a lover, but also a friend, so it is important to consider whether getting closer is right for both of you.

- Consider how your relationship could affect other friends. If your circle of friends could be changed by your relationship becoming more intimate you may want to consider how you will break the news to them. Usually in these situations the group is very accepting once they have understood why you want the change, but you should take it slowly at first. Avoid bursting in with the news. Instead, gradually tell people until it seems that your news has been accepted.

- Keep your friendship alive. This may seem advice that is out of place here, but it is easy to forget, in the thrill of falling in love, that you were friends first. Carry on doing the things you enjoyed as friends, building on these shared interests rather than dismissing them now that you are lovers. For example, if you have always enjoyed going to the local football match together, make sure this is still part of your time together. Maintain any other links with friends. Some 'friends to lovers' couples seem to cut off former friendships as they become more and more immersed with each other. But you will probably miss your mates once you are past this 'joined at the hip' phase, so keep your contacts alive if you can.

Dates with work colleagues

Now that both sexes are likely to work full time, one of the most frequent ways to meet a partner is through work. This is a natural way to meet people. After all, you may spend eight hours or more each day with a group of people who share the same kind of goals in life and are interested in similar issues to you. Among these are bound to be people who seem attractive. The television industry has certainly grasped this idea since most of our TV screens are full of people in dramas meeting lovers through work! Work can be an ideal place to build a relationship, but I would suggest that there are some areas of caution to take into account.

- Think through how your relationship may appear to other members of staff. For instance, if one of you is on a higher level than the other, it could be perceived that the person who is at a lower level will receive preferential treatment over pay or position. You must be scrupulous about observing all the workplace rules in these matters, or you could be accused of nepotism.
- Avoid displays of affection in front of others at work. It may feel natural to you, but to your workmates it could seem unprofessional and irritating. Keep work as work, and leisure as leisure.
- If you ask someone out at work (or get asked out), and they (or you) refuse, carry on behaving absolutely fairly towards one another. The same goes if you start a relationship that fails. You may find it difficult or embarrassing, but if you are to work together there must be no hint that your previous relationship alters any aspect of your professional relationship. If one of you calls off a fledgling relationship, talk about how you will handle things at work when you meet.
- If you feel a relationship is becoming more serious, and it could have an impact at work, discuss how you will deal with this.

For instance, you may wish to arrange a transfer, or talk to your boss about the two of you being a couple.

Dates with strangers

Most dates are with strangers, even if you think you already know the person. This might sound like a contradiction in terms, but the truth is that once you go on a date with someone, you will develop a perception of them that is totally different from that you previously had. For example, you may hesitate about accepting a date with a colleague at work who seems to be full of jokes and teasing, only to discover that this is a cover for a more serious and caring person beneath the banter.

But there are some dates where you will not know the person at all, and perhaps will not have any friends who know your date either. This is most obviously the case if you are meeting through a dating agency. Later in this chapter you can read about safe dating practice, but there are some special concerns for dating a stranger that you may like to consider:

- Try not to assume a special image for the night. It is tempting to dress up to the nines, but just be yourself – smart but natural – and you will give (and hopefully receive) a much truer picture than if you make a certain kind of impression when you start out, only to alter this later on.

- For a first date, you may want to meet somewhere fairly quiet. You can explore nightclubs later if you would like to, but when you are just getting to know one another, a peaceful café or restaurant is a good choice. That way, you can get to know each other without having to shout over loud music or other people.

- Avoid diving into the minutiae of your life the moment you begin to talk. You may want to tell him or her that you are returning to dating after the messy breakdown of a love affair, but this will seem like information overload to your new friend. Stick to simple information, such as your work, interests and how you chose the dating agency you did. Do not forget to ask open questions and encourage your date to tell you about himself or herself.

- If you feel that further dates are not for you, be polite at the end of the date and say something like 'I've enjoyed meeting you, but I feel it would be better if we didn't meet again.' This gives a straightforward message, rather than just avoiding answering the phone or saying yes to a date you know you will never keep. If you want to pursue the relationship, say something like 'Would you like to meet again?' This is better than 'Let's arrange another date', as it leaves room for your date to say yes or no, rather than have to find an excuse not to see you again.

Safe dating practice

Most people who go on dates with people they do not know do so in perfect safety and have a great time. But for the small minority, the experience is not so happy. You have only to look in the daily newspapers to read stories about abduction and rape. It is sensible to follow safe dating practice when you begin to go out with somebody new. You will feel more secure and your partner will realise that you are to be treated seriously. Here are some basics of safe dating:

- Always meet in a public place, close to the venue of the date.
- Make your own arrangements for travel to and from the date. Never offer or accept a lift from a date you do not know very well. If you intend to book a taxi, do so for both journeys before you meet your date.
- Make sure you have your own cash and/or credit cards. In an emergency, this may be useful as a taxi fare.
- In the early stages of a potential relationship, go for daytime dates if possible. For example, shared lunches or coffee in an attractive restaurant or walks in a park. You will feel safer if it is daylight and there are plenty of people around.
- Arrange to 'go Dutch' for the date. Some people interpret paying for a meal as an invitation to take things further.
- Do not give details of your home, telephone number or e-mail until you are very confident of the person you are meeting. Ideally, arrange further dates through the dating agency or a

friend. A mobile telephone number could be a reasonable compromise if you need to make contact with one another.

- Even if you think you are made for each other, never go back to each other's homes for a nightcap. It is too dangerous, given that some rapists can seem charming in the first instance.
- Tell someone you trust where you are going, who you are with and what time you expect to be home. Ask them to call you after this time to ensure you are safe.
- If you go for a drink together, always accompany your date to the bar and watch the drink being poured. Never accept a drink that you have not seen being poured from a third party. Always check that water bottles have not been previously tampered with. If you have any suspicions, dispose of the drink. These precautions are necessary because of the 'date rape' drug that can be poured into a drink. The drug can cause dizziness, sleepiness and paralysis. If you think it has been used, or you feel unwell, call for medical help immediately. Some rapists have used the feelings of illness as a reason to take the person to their home, giving an ideal venue for an attack to take place. It is also wise for you to check that drinks have not been spiked with extra alcohol, with the intention that you will become drunk quickly. These precautions are important if you are a woman, but can also apply to a man as it is possible for men to be raped, a fact often overlooked by men preparing to go on a date.
- Do not have sex with someone on a first date! I am sorry if this seems prudish, but you simply do not know the person well enough to judge how they might behave once you are alone. You also run the risk of catching a sexually transmitted disease (see Chapter Six for more information on sex and dating).

Internet safety

These days it is easy to develop a relationship with someone in cyberspace and imagine that they are just the one for you. But if you want to be safe there are some safety rules you should apply to contact with anyone via the net:

- Never give out details such as home telephone numbers, addresses or other personal data.
- Do not arrange to meet someone you have made contact with via the net on your own. Always go with a friend, and meet in a public place for coffee or lunch, not an evening meal.
- Tell people where you are going, even if you are with a friend.
- Never be tempted to go in a car alone with your new friend or invite them to your home in the early weeks after meeting.
- Introduce them to friends as quickly as possible. If they seem reluctant to do this, you should have alarm bells ringing.
- If anything happens that you are not happy about, walk away from the situation.
- Follow the safety rules above.

Asking for, accepting and refusing dates with dignity

Managing the beginning of a new relationship is probably the most difficult time for both partners involved. Firstly, you have to get over the nerves of approaching the person you like (or receiving an approach), deciding how to say yes or no and then making the arrangements for the date, if you do want to go. Some of this difficult experience is softened if you meet via an introduction or social agency, or through friends, but you will eventually have to make a face to face arrangement for further dates, or refuse a date. Here is some help in managing these testing events.

Asking for a date

From the outside, asking for a date might seem simple. First you identify the object of your desires, then you ask them to go for a drink with you. But this simplicity is clouded by human nature! If you decide to approach someone, you may find you ask yourself a hundred questions. Does he or she like me? What will I do if they say no? Or yes? How can I get out of the situation without embarrassment if it all goes wrong? And so on – you can probably think of lots of your own questions at this point. So here is a quick guide to asking someone out:

- Choose a place where you are not in full view of your work-mates, fellow students, friends at the tennis club etc. Your decision to ask someone out is your private business. Whether the person you approach agrees or disagrees, it is still something to be discussed between the two of you, not in a room full of other people who will probably be keen to pass an opinion on your choice, given half a chance.

- If you feel nervous about making the approach, you may find you blurt out something about going on a date before you have thought about what you really want to say. Try thinking about the words you will use, but keep it simple. Say something like 'I wonder if you would like to come to see a film/have a drink/go out for a meal with me this week?' Make sure you describe what kind of date you have in mind and the time schedule. Vague suggestions about dating 'sometime' will only leave your date wondering what exactly you are talking about and possibly how serious you are. If they respond by saying 'I need to think about it/consult my diary,' say 'When could you let me know?' Try not to be pushy or demanding, but be clear that you would like an answer as soon as possible. You could justify asking this by saying that you would like to book the tickets/table etc. If they do ask for some time to think your invitation over, do not crowd them by standing over them. Ask when it would be OK to call or talk again, and leave. Giving space in this way will help the person you want to ask out to feel that they also have space to make their own response.

- If you do not hear within the time you agreed, it is OK to make another approach, but be careful that you do not seem to be pushing the situation. Just ask politely again, and see what kind of response you get. You may have to face the fact that their prevarication is an indication that they are not interested and mark the idea down to experience.

- You can try a variation on asking directly by sending a card, e-mailing or phoning up. If you do this, follow the same rules about keeping things simple with clear directions about when you would like to go out and where. Ask for a response, either in the same medium or in person. The advantage of this is that it gives both of you 'room to breathe', and could be useful if you are really unsure of the likely response to your suggestion.

Accepting a date

You may wonder what more there can be to accepting a date other than to say 'yes'! But how you accept the date can make a difference to how you go on to set up the date together, and perhaps subsequent dates.

- If you have been asked out in a situation where you feel pressurised – perhaps because a friend has pushed you into going out with someone – give yourself some space. Suggest you discuss the date at a time to suit you, and in a place you can be comfortable with.
- If you find yourself in a very noisy environment, or do not want to be overheard by work colleagues, ask to move to a venue where this is less of a problem – even if it is only the corridor outside your office!
- Listen to how the offer is phrased, and reply to what is actually being asked. For instance, if your date says 'Would you like to go out sometime?' try to get more detail on what exactly they are suggesting. If they find this difficult to answer (don't forget, they could be very nervous) make some suggestions yourself. A shared coffee is a good start, or if you feel more confident, perhaps a meal in a restaurant. Ask them what kind of food they prefer.
- Make a note of any arrangements. It is surprising how this kind of detail slips from your mind in the heat of the moment. Do not be afraid to check out any details you have forgotten.
- Let the person asking you out know how pleased you are! I do not mean you have to throw your arms around them as this might seem a tad over the top! Instead, just say 'I'd be delighted to go out with you', or whatever comes naturally.

Refusing a date

Of all the issues you may have to manage around dating, refusing a date is potentially the most awkward. Not only will you possibly feel embarrassed at turning someone down, but they will also wonder what went wrong and feel embarrassed that they could have misjudged the situation so badly.

- If you know you want to turn someone down, and have an inkling that the approach is coming your way, try to find somewhere to talk where you will not be distracted. The same guidelines for accepting a date apply to turning someone down – be private, if possible, and without an audience of friends or workmates.
- Put yourself in the shoes of the person you are refusing. They will probably feel unhappy at your refusal, and may even press you for a reason. Stay polite and avoid making personal remarks. For example, you may know that you could never go out with someone who dresses the way they do, but telling them this, coupled with a refusal, could severely dent their self-esteem. It is worth remembering that one man's meat is another man's poison, so what you do not like, someone else could find enchanting! Say something like 'I really appreciate your offer of a meal together, and I am really flattered you asked me, but I do not feel able to accept.' Avoid prevaricating, perhaps by saying you might be free next week, when you know you do not want to go out with him or her at all. This is just unkind. Far better to be honest so they know where they stand.
- If you are asked to explain why you do not want a date, stick to saying something simple like 'I am sorry but I do not want to go into any more detail.' This should solve most enquiries, but some people are more persistent. If you meet someone like this, ask them to respect your reasons and to stop asking you for this information. Do not be tempted to go out with someone because you 'feel sorry for them' or because you think going on one date will stop them asking again. You will simply encourage them more and then find it harder to put an end to future dates.
- If you turn someone down, do not tell all your mates what you have done. If the person is inexperienced in asking someone out, or has taken ages to find the courage to approach you,

gossip about their failure will make things ten times worse. Give them some respect and you will feel better about the situation as well.

Reading the unspoken signs about your potential partner's character

When you start out on a date you may wish you had a crystal ball with you so that you could find out whether the relationship might be successful or doomed to failure! While it is not possible to make 100 per cent predictions about how a relationship might pan out there are some ways of deciding if a date is worth pursuing, or if it might be wise to call things off.

How were you asked?

As you have read above, how you are approached for a date can be very important, and tell you a lot about the kind of person you may have encountered. A sensitive approach, that allows you time and space to make a decision, indicates that your potential date is probably a caring person. If the approach was pushy or made in a jokey fashion, the person asking for the date could either be very nervous or is perhaps not treating the date in as serious a manner as you might like. Watch for a very slick approach – perhaps a practised 'line' in asking you out, or a pre-arranged date – as this could indicate that they have had a lot of casual relationships.

How do they behave with you?

You may not want a lot of stuffy formality, such as the man opening doors or seating the woman at the table, but look for politeness and interest in you as a person. Notice if they ask questions about you and encourage you to tell them about yourself (but not so much that you find yourself talking about your private life in detail) and if they tell you about their interests and so on. If they seem to shy away from particular subjects it could be worth noting this to check on if the relationship proceeds. Avoidance of a certain issue may not be sinister, but could indicate some sensitivity. For example, Leanne found that Terry avoided discussing his work with her. After several attempts to discover what he did for a living, he eventually admitted he was a mortuary attendant. Terry explained that he had told a previous date and she had eventually walked off because she could not deal with the idea that he handled dead bodies! Leanne explained that she did not feel squeamish about this, and this reassured Terry that he could be honest about his work. If your date persistently avoids answering questions, or seems uneasy about speaking personally, it could indicate that they want to hide something from you, but do not jump to conclusions too quickly.

Here are a few other signs that indicate sincerity when conversing:

- They are able to meet your gaze. Looking down or over your shoulder rather than looking at you can indicate shyness, but can also suggest that the speaker has something to hide.
- Placing a hand over the mouth or close to the lips when speaking is sometimes a sign of uncertainty or even lying.
- Sitting with arms and legs tightly crossed, or angling the body away from you, could suggest they are less interested than you might hope.
- Frequent interruptions, or talking across you, suggests he or she is not really listening to you or may be more interested in themselves than you.
- Awkward silences can come about simply because you do not know each other well, but can sometimes suggest that you are struggling to find things in common.
- Seemingly accidental brushing of hands or other kinds of brief touch, perhaps as a drink is passed, mean there is definite interest in developing the relationship, if only in the short term.
- Laughing and sharing a joke are well-known parts of human courtship behaviour. If he or she laughs with you (but not at you) they are seeking to develop the relationship.

At the end of the date, your partner may want to make arrangements to meet again, or you may wish to arrange to see him or her again. How this happens can tell you whether your date is as keen as you are.

If they ask to make an arrangement, fixing actual dates and times and double checking phone numbers with you, then they are probably very interested in seeing you again. If they casually ask for a contact number, make a vague promise to call or make no arrangements, they may not be very interested in meeting up again. This can be a tricky moment at the end of a date as neither of you may be absolutely certain if the other wants to meet up again. If you wait to be asked, you may miss out. On the other hand, if you ask to arrange a second date, and they do not want to, you could feel very embarrassed. Try asking if they have enjoyed the evening. Follow this by offering a contact number. If they want some time to decide about meeting again they can then take the number away. Ask for a contact number for you to call. To avoid the agony of waiting to see if you are called, say something like 'If we have not made contact by X day, shall we assume we will not meet again?' This gives you both an opportunity to call or not, as you decide. If your date calls you and you are not interested in meeting again, just say something simple like 'I'm sorry, I am not interested in meeting again. Thank you for a pleasant evening.' I know this all sounds very formal, and in reality things are likely to be very much more relaxed, but these guidelines can help you to survive if you find yourself floundering during a date.

Other things to look for during a first date

Here is an instant guide to the body language that you might encounter during a date:

- Leans towards you, especially with their upper body = interested and trying to gain your interest.
- Puts hands behind head, leans back = thinks they are better than you, and is seeking to impress.
- Preening (fiddling with or smoothing hair and brushing of clothes) = about to make an approach.
- Points foot towards partner, or sits with one leg over the other, knee towards partner, or angles knee towards partner = interested, but perhaps unsure of response.
- If the woman exposes her wrists and upper arms (perhaps by

pulling up sleeves or playing with a bracelet) = definite sexual interest!

- Mirroring of each other's behaviour (he leans forward, she leans forward etc) = a feeling of closeness and identification.
- Women often use the 'sideways glance' to try to interest a man = flirty behaviour designed to 'hook' the partner.
- One partner stands while the other sits = some power play, maybe because the one standing is trying to make the one sitting feel less powerful.
- Placing a hand on an arm or shoulder = territorial, probably shows a high degree of interest.
- Walking ahead, expecting the other to follow = over-confident, and possibly not very concerned about the person following.
- Stands inside the 'comfort zone' (the invisible distance zone that most people have around them). In normal life we stand about two or three feet apart from each other. Those who enter this 'comfort zone' are those most intimate to us = usually indicates that they would like to get closer, or are trying to be intimidating.

After the first date is over

Once you have been on a first date, it is important to spend some time thinking about whether you enjoyed the date, and if you want to take things further. Some people become so carried away with the idea that the other person seemed to like them that they lose sight of considering whether they liked them back! Try asking yourself the following questions to decide if you want to take things further:

What is my intuitive feeling about the date?

While I would be the last person to suggest that you should jump to conclusions, or make a snap decision on first impressions, sometimes an intuitive feeling can help you to decide if you want to meet again. Pay attention to your feelings and thoughts – did you feel comfortable, under pressure, relaxed or tense? Did the conversation flow naturally or seem very stilted? Did you *like* the person? Sometimes, these intuitive feelings are important as they form a backdrop to any other considerations you may have. If the date seemed to go well, and you would like to repeat it, then you may have the grounds for building a relationship.

Is there anything I want to change?

Obviously, if you wanted to go out with a tall man or a short woman, and were disappointed, you cannot change these facts of life. But you may feel that there were certain things that jarred with your enjoyment of the evening. For instance, Nigel felt attracted to Deidre when he went on a foursome date with her and two friends, but she spent a lot of the evening talking to her friends, leaving Nigel feeling 'out in the cold'. Nigel was not sure if this was because Deidre did not like him, was shy and talked to her friends to cover up her shyness or did not realise that he felt cut off. Nigel decided that on their next date he would ask for the two of them to go somewhere alone rather than on a double date so that he could get to know Deidre without the distraction of her friends. If there is anything you would like to change, try to find a way, like Nigel, of testing out whether this change is achievable.

What was really good about the date?

This might seem an obvious question, but if you think the date has gone really well, you may be carried away on the success of the time you spent together rather than thinking about why you were so happy. Ask yourself if you liked the way your date looked, talked to you, shared your enjoyment of the film/meal/concert, asked you about your work and so on. Look for a holistic view to emerge. It is natural for you to be excited by your date's good looks or great social manner, but if you decide to go on future dates based on just one overwhelming attribute of your potential partner you could be disappointed.

In conclusion

This chapter has dealt with the art of conversation, how to manage different types of dates and safe dating practice. You have also looked at asking for, refusing, and accepting a date. You have considered how to read the unspoken signs of dates and thought about understanding what happened on a first date, and how to decide about taking things further.

The next chapter deals with the developing intimate relationship and with managing a new sexual relationship.

6

Getting Closer –
Dating and Intimacy

There was a time when linking intimacy with a new relationship would have been frowned on – certainly it is not an issue that respectable Victorian couples would have wanted to contemplate! But we live in changed times. Becoming sexual with a date is an issue that most people have to face when thinking about the kind of partner they would like.

For some people there are significant religious and cultural reasons why sexual closeness should wait until marriage. Others may feel that they do not want to be sexual with someone until they are very sure of a mutual commitment to each other. Many people feel that becoming sexual is a natural part of a relationship, regardless of future commitment. However you feel about this issue, it is an important item to include in your reflections about what you want from a new relationship.

CASE STUDY
Judy and Lee had been going out together for three months when Lee asked Judy to go away for a weekend in a country cottage. Although they had kissed and cuddled, even caressed in each other in an intimate way, they had not had intercourse. Judy felt

confused about whether this was what she wanted as the next step in her relationship with Lee. She knew she really liked Lee, but was not sure if she loved him. For Judy, love was a crucial ingredient before sleeping with a partner. Judy had had several partners in the past, but had only had one partner she felt she had loved and had had really good sex with. She had learnt from experience that she wanted the feelings of love to be present before deciding to have sex with a partner. Lee, on the other hand, knew that he was using the weekend in a specific way. He wanted to find out how he felt towards Judy, and felt that he could not make a commitment without discovering what it would be like to spend an extended amount of time with her, including lovemaking. For Lee the weekend was an investigation into his feelings; for Judy, the weekend needed to be a celebration of commitment, not a means of discovering what they wanted from each other.

As with Judy and Lee, sexual closeness can denote different things to different people – a casual encounter or a declaration of love. If you mean one thing, while your partner means another, you may find you are on the path to confusion and communication mix-ups.

Are you ready?

Before you get to the stage of initiating or responding to sexual approaches, you need to think about whether you are ready to be close to your potential partner. You can do this whether you actually have a partner or not. In fact, asking yourself the following questions will allow you to test out your feelings and responses before you get into a relationship. This can help you to make decisions that suit you, rather than end up with a sexual relationship that 'just happens'.

What would need to happen to make me feel ready for a sexual relationship?

In answering this question there are a number of issues you should consider, such as:

Trust

This is the fundamental building block of most relationships, whether long or short term. By this I mean that you feel you can rely on the person you are with, feel that they respect your feelings and decisions and care about things that are of importance to you. If your partner keeps their promises, does not harass you into taking actions you do not want to and supports you in your endeavours, then you have the makings of a trusting relationship. This normally takes some time to achieve – months rather than weeks. This is why jumping into a sexual relationship can often cause problems, but more on this later.

Knowledge

Knowing about your partner and their circumstances can help you to feel secure in developing an intimate relationship. You may not know every detail of a partner's past when you begin a sexual relationship, but a broad understanding of their background and recent history can help you to make a judgement about the wisdom of embarking on a closer relationship. For instance, if you discovered that your partner had been through a string of lovers, often leaving them after just a few months, you would probably want to delay making a more intimate relationship until you saw evidence of a longer commitment.

Evidence

Signs that your partner sees the sexual relationship as part and parcel of the whole relationship can give you both the chance to feel that the sex is not just a kind of 'add on' – perhaps undertaken because you 'think it is time to do it' or that it is an end in itself. This is a slightly contentious issue, because some people feel that it is OK to have sex for its own sake. If you are one of these, then that it is your personal choice. But this book is aimed at meeting a partner and maintaining a relationship, and there is not much doubt that as far as a committed relationship goes, you need the sexual relationship to enhance the commitment, not detract from it. So a holistic approach to the sex can add to the pleasure of getting to know one another. In other words, talking about the possibility of sleeping together is important in order to create the feeling that you both know what you want and when. This is not to deny the importance of romantic spontaneity – just to suggest that you need to think through how a potential sexual relationship will affect you and your lover.

What do I want from a sexual relationship?

As you answer this question I am not only suggesting that you think about physical satisfaction, although this is important, but about the emotional issues that go along with a sexual relationship:

Fulfilment

This can mean not only a physical 'at oneness' from a sexual viewpoint, but also a feeling of being so close to your partner that the sex is more than just the satisfaction of your physical desires. This is a very subjective experience, and not easy to describe, but if you have ever known this particular kind of intimacy it leaves a powerful positive memory. Not all individual acts of sex live up to this feeling – sometimes the earth moves, other times it may feel like a comforting cuddle – but if overall your lovemaking helps you both to feel that you have chosen the right person then it is a strong indicator that the relationship has a future.

Shared satisfaction

This is vital to most sexual relationships. If you feel that your partner is getting more from the experience than you, or you feel guilty because you occasionally feel as if you are 'using' your partner, then this aspect of your intimate relationship will need addressing. This kind of imbalance in the relationship can come about if one of you has higher hopes of the relationship than the other – perhaps one partner wants a long-term commitment, while the other wants a fun couple of weeks together. This can make sex hard to enjoy, especially if the difference in your behaviour becomes obvious early in the sexual relationship.

Sexual compatibility

This is probably a more popular concept these days than it has ever been. The notion that two people should seek compatibility in their intimate life is quite a new idea. Previous generations have either worked out what they wanted under the cover of confidentiality, or followed what they thought of as the norms of behaviour. The old joke about women 'laying back and thinking of England' is really about what was (and maybe, in some parts of the world, still is) expected of women from a sexual standpoint. However, as we have become more open about relationships and sex, we have begun to ask if there are different ways of approaching sex that mean that some couples should not be together, purely from a sexual viewpoint. I am not sure if this is a decision that can be made, once and forever, at the start of a relationship. As a psychosexual therapist I know that most partners' experience of sex is that it changes throughout life. Certain circumstances – such as having a baby, feeling tired, suffering an illness, growing older – affect sexual enjoyment. Learning what your partner enjoys or dislikes influences intimate behaviour as you get to know each other. Even likes and dislikes can change as you feel differently towards your partner according to your emotions and circumstances. Someone who felt quite uninhibited sexually might find it hard to be so uninhibited if they discovered that their partner was having an affair, and could even decide not to have sex at all because the crucial element of trust had been lost.

Having said this, there may be certain types and combinations of sexual behaviour that would make you feel uncomfortable, even if the relationship did alter over the years. For example, Maria felt that she could no longer maintain a relationship with Connor because he wanted her to give him oral sex. Maria had been abused by her step-father in her childhood, and the act of oral sex had traumatic memories for her. Although she tried to explain to Connor, he still asked Maria for oral sex. Maria felt she could not deal with the issue every time they made love, and this, coupled with other misgivings about the relationship, made her end it.

Passion

Passion is a word that is often used to describe sex. 'Bodice ripper' novels are full of passionate embraces and thrilling sexual encounters. Certainly, most people look for a degree of passion in a sexual relationship – without it sex would be very mechanistic. But you might ask, 'What is sexual passion?' I think it is composed of several different elements. Laughter and fun lift sex to another plane altogether. If you can laugh together (but not at each other) as you make love then you are relaxed. Relaxation and a feeling of security can help passion to flourish. There should be a willingness to enter into your partner's feelings and desires, although they should respect your limitations. And a feeling of fancying your partner – perhaps an obvious one, but often overlooked when thinking about sexual behaviour. Only you know what is fanciable in another person – you may like plump women or thin men, young or old, brown or blue eyes – but you will know when that certain indefinable quality has been met. As a therapist, I often ask people what they found attractive about their partner. Here are a few answers to get you thinking about what you tend to see as attractive:

'When he smiles his eyes crinkle up – I like that.'

'I saw her bum in her tight jeans from across the bar and I knew I just had to get to know her.'

'He has a really dark brown voice.'

'She is a very kind person – I know this because I know several of her workmates, and they say exactly the same thing.'

'The way her hair hangs across her cheek really turns me on.'

'When we're together, we laugh all the time. He's so funny.'

'I couldn't take my eyes off her cleavage!'

'He has really long, slim legs.'

'She was a friend for years until one day I looked at her sitting across the table and realised she was beautiful and I had never noticed.'

'I love his hairy chest!'

How close is close?

Now that you have thought about what you want from a sexual relationship, you might like to consider how you will know when to initiate it. Reading this, you might be tempted to think that starting out on a sexual relationship is 'natural' and 'just happens'. It is true that from the outside, most sexual relationships seem to develop on a continuum. There rarely appears to be a particular moment when sex suddenly starts to happen (unless you come from a cultural or religious background that stipulates that sex should only occur in marriage). But for many couples there is often a moment when one or both partners decide they will sleep together. Sometimes one partner may call the shots, asking the other to go to bed with them. In other situations, the couple seem to come to the same idea together, and sleeping together becomes a natural next step. But there may be times when you feel unsure about whether you are ready for sex. If you are beginning dating, you may want to understand more about reading the signs of when closeness leads to intimacy. This is particularly true if you are young, perhaps still in your teens. Here are some guidelines on recognising when this has happened. Whether you then decide to go ahead and make love is, of course, up to you.

You know each other well

Although it is possible to have sex with a stranger, or leap into bed with someone after a very short time, on the whole, the better you know someone the more likely you are to have a sexual relationship that adds to the whole of the partnership. By 'know each other' I mean that you can talk easily about your life and relationship, that you feel you can trust the other person and that you know something about their life before they met you. This can happen in weeks, but is more likely to take a few months to develop.

You have moved from group dating to wanting to spend more and more time alone together

If you met via a group situation, or have always spent most of your time with a group of friends, you may notice that you seek to be alone together. The common diagnosis of love sickness about 'gazing into one another's eyes all day' may suddenly seem to describe you very well. This physical closeness and absorption in each other can indicate that your love life is beginning to take off. If you are still in your mid or late teens, now is the time to think about what you want to do. If you are a girl under the age of 16, you are under the age for consensual legal sex. I suggest you consider waiting for a while until you are older. The rate of teenage pregnancies in the UK is the highest in Europe. Talk to someone you trust about your feelings – a parent, teacher, your GP or carer – and seek their help.

You have progressed from kissing (snogging) to intimate touching

Studies on sexuality seem to suggest that most people progress through stages of intimacy before intercourse. These are:

- Kissing and cuddling. Touching, but not on breasts and genitals.
- More intense kissing, graduating to touching breasts and genitals, often over clothes at first.
- Moving towards total body contact – for example, lying down so that all the body is in contact with the partner's body. This can occur clothed or with some clothes removed.
- Progression to intimate touching, including breasts and genitals. This sometimes occurs while clothed, semi-clothed or when naked.
- Mutual stimulation of the genitals, sometimes to climax, but without intercourse.
- Proceeds to intercourse.

Most people who want to develop a relationship will take some weeks or months to progress through these stages, although it can depend on the age of the person, and whether they have had previous experience in intimate relationships. The reasons why some people move through all these stages in one night – having one night stands or flings – are varied. Intense feelings of 'this is the one' can cause a couple to abandon the process described above, going straight to intercourse. Others will have natural inhibitions removed by alcohol or drugs. Whatever the reason, from a long-term-relationship point of view, it is usually better to approach developing a sexual relationship in stages. This is because if you have intercourse very quickly you will be doing so when you know very little about each other, and what kind of relationship you are likely to have in the future. This is akin to diving into the deep end of a swimming pool to discover if you can swim! If you want to learn to swim, it is better to start in the shallow end until you have gained your confidence. The same is true of developing a sexual relationship. In order to feel comfortable about intimacy with a partner, you need to pass through the different stages, pausing after each one, in order to assess if you want to take things further.

You feel secure with your partner

Although it is not strictly necessary to have a relationship completely sorted out in order to have a sexual relationship, it is helpful if you feel secure and settled. If you reach a stage where you feel that you can trust your partner and know they are unlikely to let you down, then going on to make love will feel right. Insecurity, and a fear that your partner will leave unless you make love, is no basis for sex. This is a form of emotional blackmail, and is an indicator that neither of you is really ready for sex, rather than a sign that you are ready to go on to a more intimate relationship. Feeling secure with a partner is particularly important if you have had a relationship where you felt unhappy in the past. If you have suffered any kind of sexual trauma, or been betrayed by a partner, it is right that you should take your time to become sexual with a new partner. If they care about you they should understand that you are moving at a pace that is right for you.

How to say yes, and when to say no

Once you have decided that you might want to begin a sexual relationship you may wonder how you can raise the issue of this with a partner, or what to say in response to a partner who asks for a sexual relationship (as in the above case study of Judy and Lee). Sometimes neither of you will be conscious of a formal 'question' being asked. You will begin to be more intimate, until one day you will realise that you are now making love. But as I suggested above, you are likely to realise that feelings about intimacy are intensifying and that the moment is coming when you will need to make a decision. Sometimes this is easy. You simply say yes! Before you reach this situation you will probably have thought about the security of the relationship and what you want from the future. But if you want a more formal way of beginning or progressing a sexual relationship, here are some ideas:

- Arrange a night away in a hotel or other venue. It would be sensible to check out that your partner feels ready for this step prior to booking, but going away can be a lovely way to get closer without the distractions of everyday life.
- Have a special evening out, making sure that your bedroom looks attractive to return to. Candles, soft lights and music will make the event memorable.
- Tell your partner how much they mean to you and ask them if they feel the same. If they do, ask them to stay the night.
- Send a small gift or card asking your partner to stay the night with you.
- Spring a surprise day out, finishing at your home so that you can move into lovemaking with you both feeling close to one another.

These ideas are great if you both know that you want to make love, but what if you are not at all sure that sex is the right next step? Saying no to someone needs careful handling. They will need to know that you are saying no to the increase in intimacy, but not necessarily to them as a person. It may be that the speed of the closeness has taken you by surprise, and you are not ready to sleep with someone you do not know very well. Or that you want to wait until you are surer of your commitment to the relationship. Whatever your reason, here are some guidelines on saying 'no' or 'not yet'.

- The simplest way to pause or stop the progression of a sexual relationship is to be honest with your partner. It is not necessary to go into great detail at first. Just say 'I would like to wait a while before we move on to lovemaking' or 'I do not want to make love.' This second answer should be used in situations where you feel under any kind of pressure (this applies equally to men and women). If you are faced with this, you must give a really clear message or your partner may think there is a chance of you changing your mind if they press you.
- If you want some time to think about whether you want a sexual relationship, ask for this. Your partner may ask you to give reasons, so think how you will phrase this. For instance, if you have experienced difficulties in the past because of making love too quickly in relationships, explain this or if you feel you need more evidence of commitment, be straightforward about saying this. I cannot stress too strongly – if your partner cares about and respects you they will honour your need to delay.
- Be understanding about how your partner may feel. If you are out of sync on this issue – he or she wants to become more intimate, while you want to slow things down – they may feel that you are really saying 'I want out of this relationship.' Reassure them that you care about them, and want to continue the relationship (if you do), but that you need more time to decide about sex.
- If you ask for a period of time to think about whether you want to go on to make love, be sure to tell your partner when you have come to a decision. It is not fair to keep a partner hanging on for your decision. In some circumstances, you may like to give an idea of how long you may need to think things through, but be wary of becoming tied down to a particular

time period as it can feel like the sword of Damocles suspended over the relationship.

If you have serious doubts about the wisdom of going on to a sexual relationship, it is far better to say no. You may feel that you want to say yes to remove any underlying tension between the two of you, or to please your partner, but making a decision based on this often sets up long-lasting feelings of regret, or even blame, that can eat away at a relationship, thereby destabilising its future.

Safer sex – what you should know

If you are starting a relationship with a new partner it is important that you follow safe sex recommendations. This is true even if you think you know your partner well. The risk of contracting a sexually transmitted infection is still high, not to mention the risk of becoming accidentally pregnant. It is possible to enjoy a loving and passionate love life while taking steps to practise safe sex. Here are the best ways to practise safe sex:

- Talk to your new partner about their sexual history. You may not get all the details from them, but it can be helpful to know whether they have had many partners or a few. Knowing this is not a defence against using safe sex, however. But it could help you to make a judgement about how you feel you should approach initiating sex and safe sex practice.
- There are several **high risk** sexual activities that can lead to the passing on of sexually transmitted infections:
    Vaginal intercourse without a condom.
    Anal intercourse with or without a condom.
    Oral sex.
    Any sexual activity that causes bleeding – either accidentally or on purpose, such as scratching, for instance.
    Sharing sex aids.
    Inserting fingers into the vagina or anus.

When making love it is *essential that you always use a condom*.

Carry them with you and make sure you can reach them easily when you start to make love. This applies to both men and women. Carrying a condom in a pocket or handbag does not make you 'a loose woman' or 'a man gagging for sex'. It means you are sensible and prepared. Learn how to put on a condom. (Men can do this when masturbating; women who have never put on a condom can learn by using a banana or cucumber for practice. Follow the instructions on the packet until you feel confident.)

- There are some other sexual activities that carry a **lower risk** of infection. They are:

  Vaginal sexual intercourse, using a condom.

  Love bites.

  Mouth to mouth kissing. (Avoid this if either partner has cuts in the mouth or bleeding gums.)

  Oral sex using a condom.

I have no doubt that you will have read or heard these safe sex messages before. But before you tell yourself you have heard it all before, please take note of them again. They really can make the difference between health and illness, and in some cases, life and death. Please do not become complacent and think that it can never happen to you. It can. Protect yourself and your sex life will be much more successful because you will feel relaxed rather than tense and anxious about the possible dangers ahead.

Safe sex is not only about taking the precautions above. It is also a by-product of thinking through your personal approach to sex, and how you feel about beginning your sex life with a new partner. Much of what I have already covered in this chapter has been concerned with helping you to decide what you want to happen from a sexual point of view. These approaches contribute to your enjoying sex, instead of worrying that you have made the wrong decisions about your choice of partner or the timing of when you will decide to make love. Here is an instant checklist of some of the points you should take into consideration when thinking about starting a new sexual relationship:

Feel ready
Never go into a sexual relationship simply to please your partner, or because you feel under pressure.

Take your time
Most people who race into sexual relationships regret taking this action. Sometimes the decision to have sex is fuelled by alcohol and/or drugs. The partner who seemed very attractive at midnight can look much less attractive in broad daylight when you are sober.

Feel safe
Make sure you follow safe dating practice (see above) and get to know your partner before deciding about making a sexual relationship.

Be intuitive
Listen to your gut feelings sometimes. I am not suggesting you necessarily act on your impulses, but you may have an instinctive feeling that someone is trustworthy or dangerous by attending to your intuition.

Look at the whole relationship
You may want to sleep with someone, but know in your heart that the rest of the relationship is wanting. Or you could feel that because the general relationship is good, it is the right time to have sex. Try to think about the sex in the context of the whole relationship.

Deciding when and how you want to create a sexual relationship with a partner is very important. But there are some other considerations that may also influence how you handle your intimate partnership. The next section looks at how you can integrate your close relationship into everyday life.

The impact on others

It may seem like a contradiction in terms to suggest that something as private and intimate as a sexual relationship can have an impact on those around you, but this is the case. What you actually do with one another is, of course, up to you. But the way in which you handle the relationship – where it takes place, when you meet and whether others approve of your behaviour – can certainly affect other people. Here are some areas where the instigation of a sexual relationship can affect others, directly or indirectly.

Children you have by a previous relationship or marriage

As a counsellor I have often heard couples tell of the problems they have encountered in trying to develop a sexual relationship with a new partner. Most people do not want the added complication of bringing a new partner into their children's lives until they are fairly sure that the relationship has some longevity. The chief difficulty with beginning a sexual relationship is that you may feel OK about this some time before you would want to make your children aware of the developing relationship. This leaves you with the difficulty of having a boyfriend or girlfriend to stay overnight, or staying with them and then explaining to the children (and perhaps the babysitter, especially if this is a family member) where you were all night! This can be a tricky problem to manage, so here are some guidelines to help you manage the situation:

- At the start of the intimate relationship, avoid bringing a lover home to be discovered in the morning by your children. If possible, ask an understanding friend to look after your children, or arrange to meet during the day when children are at school. If you need a babysitter, choose someone who is understanding and sympathetic to your new relationship. Explain why you need their support. You will find that if you are relaxed about who is looking after your children, your new sexual relationship will be much easier.

- If you have no alternative but to bring your lover into the home, pave the way to them staying the night by inviting them to meet the children. For instance, invite them to come for coffee on a Saturday, graduate to a film or video shared together, followed by a meal for just the two of you while the children go to bed. The idea is to take the 'getting to know you' process in steps. The worst possible scenario is for the children to discover your lover in bed with you one morning. This can be a real shock to a child who may already have had to come to terms with the loss of a parent (through death or divorce). I have met many couples who felt this was a 'natural' way to allow the children to learn about a new relationship but, in reality, it is usually an extremely painful way to learn about a parent's new love.

- Older children often find the whole notion that a parent wants or enjoys sex hard to come to terms with, or even laughable! You may have to overcome some resistance from a teenager about your lover. One way to get round this is to talk to them about your strong feelings for the new person in your life. Explain they are becoming important to you, and you may want them to stay overnight sometimes. You should also employ the 'staged introduction' that applies to younger children (see above). Do not make the mistake of imagining that because the teenager is older they are less sensitive to changes in parental relationships. They also need consideration and careful handling if you want a relationship that is not characterised by your children trying to split you from your latest love.

- Use the same consideration towards the children of your lover. Imagine how it might feel for them as you enter their life. Even if your new partner presses you to stay the night, think hard about how this could influence his or her children. It is true that you cannot take responsibility for all their responses and that, as their parent, your lover should make suitable arrangements for them if you stay overnight, but you should take some responsibility for caring for their well-being.

Parents and other relatives

You may wonder how your sexual relationship and choice of partner could possibly affect your relatives. I can hear you saying 'this is a private matter'! But the truth is that many people do find that even their most intimate relationships are affected by the attitudes of their nearest and dearest. For example, Kevin had moved back to live with his widowed mother while his house was receiving a complete 'make-over' after a flood had devastated the ground floor. Just before the flood occurred, Kevin had met a new girlfriend, Sasha. As the relationship developed, he began to bring her home. Kevin's mother, Jill, took a dislike to Sasha, and definitely disapproved of Sasha staying the night. She began to make her feelings known by telling Sasha about Kevin's previous girlfriends, whom she had preferred. Kevin and Sasha had several arguments about what was happening, and their relationship almost faltered. Fortunately, Kevin's home reclamation and repair was finished in the nick of time and they were able to restore their partnership, although Kevin was still left trying to bridge the rift between Jill and Sasha.

Managing how parents respond to a partner can be affected by whether your parents expect you to have a partner of the same religious or ethnic background, or if they find it hard to cope with you being gay or developing a relationship with someone who is older or younger than you. If you counter your parents or relatives in some way, the guilt or secrecy can cause real problems in a sexual relationship – sometimes leading to erection difficulties in men or lack of libido in women. Here are some guidelines on managing these issues:

- As with the previous section on children, make a gradual introduction of your new partner to relatives. Invite them for a meal or on an evening out with your new love. Expecting them to put up with a new partner when they hardly know them is unfair and could lead to a more serious breakdown in communication.
- If you meet resistance to a partner from family members, especially when the sexual relationship begins, it may seem

tempting to disregard your relatives' opinion. But it might be wise to ask yourself why they seem to oppose your new love. Sometimes other family members can detect potential difficulties that you may have missed in the heady phase of first love. Even if you disagree with their analysis, taking their opinion seriously can help to maintain a flow of conversation about the relationship which can stand you in good stead if you decide the relationship is to be more committed. Slamming an emotional door on your family can often cause a great deal of unhappiness and regret later on.

- Talk the relevant family members through your reasons for wanting to develop a relationship with a particular partner. I am not suggesting you tell them all the details of your intimate life, but explaining why you feel as passionately as you do can help them to see things from your point of view.

Friends and other members of your social circle

Friends are often the first to have an opinion about your choice of partner, and often quite forward about letting you know their feelings! Sometimes these opinions will be very welcome. Gary found this when he began dating Tina: their mutual friends agreed that they were made for each other, and had been pushing them together behind the scenes for months! Or their views may be at variance with how you feel: Fiona felt upset that her best friend Davina objected to her choice of boyfriend, especially as Davina had suggested that Fiona should go out with the boy in question. You may also fear losing close friends if you spend a great deal of time with a new date, and this is especially relevant when you begin a sexual relationship, as your strong feelings at this phase could block your desire to spend time with your mates. Use the following to help you keep your friendships and your new relationship alive:

- Spend time with your friends away from your new love. Put aside an evening or other appropriate meeting time and enjoy all the things you have previously enjoyed. Reassure them that you still care about them.

- Introduce your new date to your friends. I suggest you do this in a group setting rather than asking your friends to meet your date individually. If there is any danger of jealousy over who has met your new partner before others, a group setting can help all your friends to feel equally valued.
- Be prepared for your date and some of your friends not to hit it off in the way that you hope. This does not mean you should abandon your date or your friends, just that you need to give both sides time to get to know one another and develop a friendship of their own.
- Remember, if the relationship fails, you may need the support of your friends to see you through, so keep your usual friendships alive; they can act as a support during successful and unsuccessful partnerships.

When sex is a problem

Most people encounter some sexual concerns at some point in a relationship. Difficulties can often follow after a particular life stage, such as childbirth or a change of work pattern. Tiredness and anxiety can also diminish sexual appetite and response. At the start of a sexual relationship there are often specific problems that people encounter, but find it hard to talk about, even to each other. It may seem odd to imagine that a new intimate relationship can run into difficulties because this is the phase that the majority of people think of the most romantic, most spontaneous and most exciting. Here are some common myths about new sexual relationships:

Myth 1: At the start of a new sexual relationship, the couple are so in tune with one another that the sex is wonderful

This myth is responsible for many a problem between new lovers. If their experience of making love is less than great they may think that this is a strong indicator that the relationship is going nowhere. More usually, the difficulties of getting to know each other, overcoming any embarrassment at becoming sexual, managing contraception, and deciding when and where to make love, can make early sexual encounters a bit hit and miss! There may be nothing wrong with your relationship that some improved communication and practice cannot put right. If you find that your first lovemaking sessions are not going as you hope, try these ideas:

- Make sure you feel relaxed and set the scene with low lighting and soft music. Find a time when you can avoid worrying that your flatmate is about to return home, and give yourselves plenty of time to enjoy getting to know each other.
- Tell your partner what you enjoy as you are making love, and ask him or her what they enjoy. Try not to be critical, as this can ruin the atmosphere and make your partner feel that they are useless. Instead, place their hand where you like to be touched and encourage them to do the same. If you really dislike something that they are doing, talk about this at some other time in a friendly (rather than accusative) manner.
- Remember, you do not have to go straight to sexual intercourse (the emotional equivalent of 0 to 60 in 10 seconds!) once you become intimate. Begin with touching and cuddling, making your way to full intercourse over a period of time. This can be a valuable way of finding out what your partner likes and dislikes, allowing you both to 'enjoy the journey as well as the arrival'.

Myth 2: New lovers are usually both ready for sex at the same time in a relationship, and this happens naturally

Myth two is responsible for lots of problems in new relationships. It is not true that a couple magically key into each other's readiness for sex, falling into each other's arms as violins play in the background. More often, one partner wants to begin lovemaking before the other partner feels ready. If the first partner wrongly assumes the other is ready, and attempts to have sex, the relationship can quickly become awkward. If the suggestion of sex has come as a real surprise to one partner, they may wonder if they have misread the situation in some way. Here are some ways of creating a mutual readiness for intimacy:

- Don't jump your partner. Test out the ground by talking about the relationship, telling your partner how special they are and being affectionate. Watch to see how your partner responds. If they seem cooler than you or less responsive than you expected, wait a while before developing a sexual relationship.
- If you are not ready for lovemaking, tell your partner in a clear way. If you hedge or make an excuse they could imagine that you might change your mind in half an hour, when you think it could be in three months' time! Just say 'I'm sorry, I'm not ready for sex in our relationship yet.' If they care for you, they will respect your wishes. If you are pushed or cajoled into sex when you have already said no, the relationship may not be right for you. Think about what *you* want and need, rather than what your partner is asking for.

Myth 3: Becoming sexual with a partner can make a dodgy relationship better

It is not unusual to find that one or both partners in an insecure relationship decide to have sex. This amounts to an attempt to superglue the partnership together through sex and usually has the opposite effect – the relationship falls apart. This is because the sex ups the pressure that the couple feel, demanding more of them, often at a time when they want to relieve pressure rather than build it up. If you recognise yourself in this scenario, here is how to avoid it in the future:

- Ask yourself why you are starting a sexual relationship when you already feel unsure about the general relationship. Instead of moving to the bedroom, ask your partner about their hopes for the future.
- For some couples, sex is the only thing that unites them. It can provide a smokescreen against parting long after the real sense of closeness has died (this can sometimes be seen in couples after a break-up, when sex continues despite the knowledge that the relationship is over). Face the reality about

the possibility of breaking up and the sexual attraction will fade.

- Sex can have a healing effect – after a minor argument, for instance – but it does not work if one or both of you realise that the relationship is in serious trouble. You are likely to end up full of regret if you sleep with someone you know in your heart is wrong for you.

When sex goes wrong

At the start of a sexual relationship there are some specific difficulties that you may encounter. Here is a list of the most common, with some solutions:

For men
Erectile problems

As a precautionary measure, it is a good idea to check out any difficulties with erections with your GP, but some erectile difficulties can be associated with the nervousness of starting a new relationship. This can be especially true if you have recently been through the difficult break-up of a previous relationship and feel uncertain about dating and/or a new sexual relationship. The development of trust and commitment can be a crucial aid to achieving erections. Some simple steps can help erectile problems that are caused by anxiety:

- Take time to relax before making love. If you are with your partner, listen to some soothing music together and give each other a massage. If you are alone, perhaps waiting for your partner to arrive, switch off from work and relax in a warm shower or bath.
- Ask your partner to touch and caress you all over. While she or he does this, allow your mind to concentrate on the sensual feelings. Try not to concentrate on any previous loss of erection. Just enjoy the sensations for what they are. Using massage oil can help make this experience even nicer.
- Allow your partner to caress your penis while you remain

relaxed, lying on your back. Again, let the erotic sensations fill your body and mind. Concentrating on the 'here and now' can make a real difference to achieving erection. Ask your partner to use oil or a lubricant such as KY Jelly to help intensify the feelings. (Be careful about highly scented oils as they can sting delicate areas. If in any doubt, a little olive oil is safe.)

If you want more help with erection difficulties, think about seeing a psychosexual therapist. See your GP for a check up and referral if the problem persists.

Premature ejaculation

Premature ejaculation is probably the most common of the difficulties that men encounter in a new sexual relationship. The combination of the excitement of a new relationship, nerves about 'getting it right' with a new partner and the thrill of seeing a partner naked for the first time, can cause a man to 'come' much more quickly than he or his partner are happy with. Here are some guidelines to help diminish premature ejaculation:

- Forget some of the old methods that are frequently used to delay an ejaculation – such as counting, remembering football teams or concentrating on non-sexual images. If you keep doing these you will eventually desensitise yourself to sexual stimulation, as well as spoiling a very intimate moment between you and your partner.
- Relax while making love, and allow your partner to caress you all over. Enter into the erotic sensations and spend plenty of time arousing your lover.
- If you sense you are getting close to the point of no return, ask your partner to stop stimulation for a while. Don't worry, your desire will return. If you would find it easier, use a pre-agreed sign that you want a 'rest'. Once the immediate sensations have died down, go back to stimulation. This may seem false at first, but it can have a miraculous effect on premature ejaculation. You can also try the 'squeeze' technique, where your partner squeezes the head of the penis firmly when you feel the desire

to come, but this is not as successful long-term as the stop-start method described above.

For women
Orgasm difficulties

It is not uncommon for a woman to find herself unable to achieve an orgasm at the start of a new relationship. Most women would say that the ability to achieve an orgasm is linked to trust in a committed relationship, although it is perfectly possible for women to have an orgasm in other situations. Here are some first steps to take towards achieving orgasm:

- Relax with your partner before making love. Enjoy a meal together or a glass or two of wine (but no more, or the evening could find you both asleep instead of in a passionate embrace!). Ask your partner to caress and touch you all over, perhaps by giving you a massage.
- If you know you would like a particular kind of stimulation, ask your partner for this, or show him or her by placing your hand over theirs. Remember that most women need direct stimulation of the clitoris to achieve orgasm, and many women find that this does not happen during intercourse. Try to use a position that allows you or your partner to continue to arouse you while you have intercourse.
- Practice self-stimulation to orgasm when alone. If you can discover what you enjoy, you can go on to share this with a partner. If you find this difficult, consider using a vibrator to help you.

Painful sex

When a new relationship becomes sexual a woman can sometimes find that feeling nervous about sex creates tension. If she is tense, this can inhibit the natural production of lubrication from the vagina. This, in turn, can make sexual intercourse very uncomfortable. Tackle painful sex by:

- Relaxing before and during sex. Make sure there has been

plenty of mutual caressing and stimulation (at least half an hour) before going on to intercourse.

- Use a lubricant such as KY Jelly. If you are going through the menopause, consult your GP, as a dry vagina can be a side effect of the menopause in some women.
- Avoid making love when you feel unsure about a relationship. If you have any doubts about going on to make love, say you would rather wait until the relationship is on a firmer footing. Anxiety is one of the chief causes of painful or uncomfortable sex.

Key elements in a sexual partner

There are some important characteristics that you should look for in a lover. These indicate a partner who is willing to care for you and make sex an integral part of the relationship. They are:

- A caring and respectful attitude towards you. If you say no, they will respect this and never push you to make love if you oppose the idea.
- They do not play 'power games' with sex, using it as a way to manipulate you in the relationship.
- A willingness to consider your particular sexual preferences, and to take these into account when making love. However, they are also able to voice their own preferences, and sometimes say no if they do not want to do something you suggest. This indicates a strong sense of self-esteem which is important in maintaining a couple relationship.
- Is able to laugh with you in bed (but not at you) and you feel able to share fun as well as passion.
- They are appreciative of your body and tell you how lovely you are. (Some poor lovers criticise their partner, even during lovemaking.)
- They take safe sex practices seriously, and never try to make you take a risk.
- They see sex as part of the relationship rather than an end in itself.

A word on holiday flings

Some new sexual relationships are born (and die) on holiday. Relationships on holiday can seem very attractive because of the circumstances. You are relaxed and probably feel almost like a different person. You will be enjoying a different routine, eating different foods and drinking (sometimes more than is good for you). All of this together tends to lower inhibitions. This can make a holiday romance seem extremely attractive. But you need to decide if the holiday romance is right for you using the same checks and balances described in this chapter. Most people do not intend to commit to a long-term relationship as a result of a holiday romance (although some people do stay with the lover they met on holiday) but it is crucial you use safe sex practices and operate the safe dating practice described above. With inhibitions lowered, you may forget or push to the back of your mind these important messages, but you need them more, not less.

In conclusion

This chapter has been chiefly concerned with making sense of sexual relationships in the context of a new partnership. It has explored the readiness for a sexual relationship, both personal and joint; what the individual may want and look for from a sexual relationship; judging the moment for intimacy, and especially how to say yes or no to a sexual relationship. It has also covered safe sex practice and how to implement this in a new sexual relationship, together with the possible impact on others of beginning a sexual relationship and some common sexual problems at the start of a sexual relationship.

7

The Future of Your New Relationship

The aim of this book up to now has been to help you find and develop a new relationship with a new partner. But finding and beginning to date a new partner is just the start of the story in relationship terms. It may feel as if, having found a new partner, all the hard work is over, but in fact it is only just beginning!

This chapter is about how to maintain a new relationship, or, in some circumstances, how to end a new relationship. The early phase of all new relationships is the most crucial as it lays down building blocks for what is to come. To borrow an old cliché, in relationship terms it is important to 'start as you mean to go on'. This does not mean that you should dig yourselves into a certain style of behaving with a partner and stay that way for years to come – simply that what you establish after this first phase of being together is built on what you have already shared.

The stages of new relationships

Most new relationships pass through stages of development. You may recognise some of them, or feel that you have not been in any relationship long enough to have met them all. Here are the most common:

Meeting

This phase is the one where you get to know each other. It might also be called the 'exploration' phase, as you grow in understanding about the kind of person you have met and become closer to.

Feeling closer

This is the stage that many people really enjoy about a new relationship. It is the stage at which you cannot wait to see each other again, feel that your new partner is the greatest thing since sliced bread and generally wonder how the world turned before you met! It can be a time of heightened sensation and very exciting. It may also have an air of unreality about it. This is usually because you have yet to know the whole of your partner, or may be projecting your own ideals about what and who your partner is.

Learning about your partner

After the thrill of developing your relationship, this stage can feel something of a let-down. You may decide you feel less keen on a partner than you first thought, or learn something about their character or personality that does not fit with your dreams of the perfect relationship. This stage can often prompt couples to split up because they compare it unfavourably with the excitement of earlier stages. But if you can stay with a partner through this stage, you may find that the relationship is more mature and satisfying because you will know your partner well and feel more confident.

Being together

If you have survived the ups and downs of the last three stages, this stage can seem like a plateau. You may feel that the relationship has 'found its own level' and you are both comfortable with both the positive and negative aspects of each other's characters. This plateau phase can act as a step to greater closeness and a real ability to trust how your partner will behave. Once you have established trust in this way, you have the key to the door of the future of your relationship.

CASE STUDY

Tanya and Ben met through a group of friends who all supported a local rugby team. Tanya had recently broken off an engagement and was looking to boost her social life, but not necessarily to find a new partner. Ben had been without a girlfriend for some time, but was happily living a bachelor lifestyle. It was something of a surprise to them both to find that they were attracted to one another. At a rugby club dinner, they were seated next to each other, and discovered that they could not stop talking to one another! Tanya thought that Ben was funny and interesting, as well as physically fit and sexy. Ben thought that Tanya was full of fun and easy to talk to. It seemed an added bonus that he considered her a pretty woman. They quickly decided to meet for a date, and spent the next two months going to movies, enjoying meals together and, of course, watching rugby. Tanya felt very attracted to Ben, and found herself looking forward to dates with great excitement. Ben was also very keen on Tanya, and found himself thinking about spending holidays with her in the coming year. Then things began to go wrong. Ben found Tanya's habit of arriving late for everything drove him mad, especially when they missed a coach that was taking them to a rugby match he had booked tickets for. Tanya also felt that Ben had a short fuse sometimes, often arguing about issues she felt were unimportant. For a few weeks, they spent less time with one another, and communication cooled. Tanya still felt interested in Ben and really missed him, while Ben still felt that Tanya was very special. Neither was too sure how to retrieve the situation when they were both invited to a friend's wedding. At the reception, they danced together and talked about what had happened to them. Tanya acknowledged that her timekeeping was dreadful, while Ben admitted he sometimes allowed himself to get riled at things that did not really matter. After the reception they went back to Ben's flat and stayed the night together. Over the coming weeks they gradually found that they could be friends and lovers, accepting each other's foibles and weaknesses. Eventually they moved in together and they married a year later.

Ben and Tanya illustrate the different phases of a growing relationship, and how it is possible to experience emotional ups and downs, but still feel strong affection for a partner. In fact, the better you can cope with change, the more successful your relationship will be. Understanding that your partner is not perfect, and may sometimes differ from you, is part of learning about adult relationships.

Strategies to survive the different stages of a new relationship

Stage One
You can maximise the meeting stage by spending plenty of time listening to and asking questions of your new friend. Find out about them, and tell them anything interesting about yourself. Try not to throw too much information at them, or interrogate them, but allow a free exchange of information as much as possible. This can often feel more natural in a group situation.

Stage Two
In this stage, you are likely to feel deeply attached or in love with a partner. This is the stage that most people recognise as 'being in love', although it can be deceptive. Some people are really in lust, not love! But this stage can be really passionate and exciting, so keep momentoes of your strong feelings for one another. Take photos, write love letters or cards and talk about how you feel about one another. The memory of this time will see you through the tougher stage you are about to encounter.

Stage Three
In this stage you will feel like a boat tossed on stormy seas. You may even wonder if the relationship can survive. Some do not, and this is probably an indicator that it lacked the strength to

carry on in the face of a challenge. Instead of looking at your partner's imperfections and wondering if you can cope, think about them as part of a wider picture of their character. In this way you can celebrate the things you like and try to accept those that are less palatable. If you are really struggling to accept something, think about how this might be changed. In Tanya and Ben's case, Tanya agreed to work on her poor timekeeping, while Ben took a relaxation class to prevent him becoming so stressed about small things.

Stage Four

In this stage, you are more settled and secure. It is a good time to take decisions about moving in together, what you want from the future of the relationship or promising a commitment. Plan how you might manage difficult issues and talk about your dreams for the two of you. If you want to change some aspect of the relationship, now is a good time to try out these changes together as you will feel more like a team and less like two individuals pulling in different directions.

What do I want now?

Once you have come through the early stages of getting to know each other, you need to think about what you want from the relationship in the near future. Fill out the following chart to help you think about what you should maximise or minimise in your new relationship:

Possible want	Very important	Of some importance	Not important
Commitment for long term			
Commitment for shorter term (less than a year)			
Sexual relationship			

Possible want	Very important	Of some importance	Not important
Shared socialising with friends of either of us			
More dates alone			
Better communication skills			
To meet family of new partner			
To discuss living together			
To know more about my new partner's past			
To spend more time getting to know each other			

Work your way down the chart, ticking the most appropriate box for each subject in the left hand column. (You may want to add some subjects of your own.) Once you have filled in the columns, look at your answers. Look first of all at those that are very important to you. For instance, you may have ticked those connected to commitment. This could indicate that you are looking beyond the relationship as it is today to something much more fixed and firm. If you ticked the 'very important' box for the column connected to 'spending time getting to know each other' this might indicate that you are still at an early stage, learning about your partner.

This exercise can help you because you can make some decisions about what you are looking for, and where you are in the four stages outlined above. It could be interesting to ask your new partner to also complete the chart, and then compare any differences you discover. For instance, you could find that one of you is looking for a long-term commitment, while the other is looking for a shorter-term commitment. This may not spell the end of the relationship, but could indicate that you need to discuss what you are both hoping for in the future. In this example, it may be that the partner who is looking for a shorter-term commitment is actually asking for time to decide on what they want. They may be willing to commit to a long-term relationship after a few months have passed.

The following are some scenarios to help you think about what you want for the future.

You want the relationship to end

Having met a new partner, you may feel intuitively that the relationship has no real future. If you have discovered that you have little in common, find talking to one another difficult, are opposed by friends and/or family or lack sexual chemistry, then it may be best to end the relationship. It can be a problem if one of you feels this way, while the other would like to continue the relationship. This is rather like trying to ride a two-wheeled bike with a wheel missing. It might be possible to drag the bike along a short way, but ultimately you would have to abandon the exercise. If you are sure the relationship is over, it is kinder to finish it completely than make promises you cannot keep about meeting in the future.

You want to develop the relationship further before you make a final decision about committing to it

The speed at which new relationships proceed is different. Some people make their minds up about a partner very quickly, while others take their time. (This can vary from partnership to partnership as well.) If you want to learn more about your partner, or get the feel of how you are together, this is better than hiding any doubts or second thoughts you may have. If your partner is speedier than you about deciding they want a commitment, ask for some weeks or months to allow you to make up your mind. Do not give an open-ended amount of time in which you will make your decision, such as 'in a while' or 'when I feel more confident about things'. This is unfair to your partner, and will only lead them to press you for a decision more urgently. Answer their enquiries honestly and with understanding.

You would like to cool the relationship down

This decision can often follow a period of intensity that took you both by surprise. Sometimes the desire to cool a relationship down follows sexual passion, perhaps after a meeting that was followed very swiftly by a sexual relationship but not the development of a general partnership in which to 'anchor' the sex. If you want to cool the relationship, avoid taking the coward's way out by not answering phone calls or messages. Face the truth and tell your partner that you want a period of re-evaluation. They may find this difficult, but if you explain that some emotional space will help you work out what you really want for the future, and that this will ground the relationship, avoiding it falling apart in the future, they should be sympathetic.

You would like to develop a relationship more quickly

If you feel a relationship has been slow to take off, you may want to intensify it. A slow start is sometimes brought about by long travelling distances between you, uncertainty about whether you want a new relationship at all (often the case if you are returning to dating after a divorce or bereavement) or simply lack of time to meet regularly. To speed things up, try to meet more often, allowing plenty of time to talk and really get to know each other. For instance, Fran and Lawrence decided to stop dating at movies, although they were both avid film fans, and meet at a country pub where they could talk to each other at length. Be wary of pushing a reluctant partner into meeting in this way in the hope that they will be 'kick started' into wanting more from the relationship. In this instance, it is better to give some space for them to decide what they want. In fact, added pressure is more likely to turn them off.

Both of you definitely want the relationship to continue

Of all the options open to you, this is probably the most straight-forward. You may come to this decision quickly, feeling a real and instant attraction to another. This is the 'glance across a crowded room' feeling – that somehow this person is a soul-mate. Alternatively, the growing realisation that you are right for each other may have developed slowly over a period of weeks or months. In this situation, it can be easy to make an assumption that your new partner feels exactly the same. Even if all the evidence points this way, make time to talk about your strong feelings towards each other as this will help to cement your relationship, as well as being a cause for celebration.

Building on strengths, solving problems

As you develop your new relationship you will want to look at it 'in the round'. You may already be aware that there are things you really like and some you are not so happy with. Some couples make the mistake of believing that these two parts of their life together are unchangeable, but this is not the case. You can work on strengths to make them even more satisfying, enjoyable and supportive as well as tackling problems in order to improve the relationship and avoid sabotage further down the line.

Build on strengths

A good start to building up those things you are already very happy about is to talk to your partner about what they are! This might seem obvious, and in fact most new lovers do create a 'mutual admiration society' by telling each other how great they are and how lucky they are to have found each other. You can formalise this process by actually listing all the things you want to celebrate.

Find a large piece of paper and some coloured pens and have a relationship 'brain storming' session. Call out and write down anything you are especially happy about in the relationship. You do not have to write in neat sentences; just put down a word or phrase that encapsulates what you want to say.

CASE STUDY

Clare and Lewis undertook this exercise three months after they met. They had fallen for each other in a short time, and were really enjoying each other's company. Here are some of the things they put in their list:

We like ten pin bowling
Our dogs like each other!
We laugh at the same jokes
I love your body
We can talk about anything
You are a caring person
Your e-mails make me laugh!
I feel I can trust you
We keep our promises
We share the same set of friends
You know just what I like to eat
We enjoy clubbing together
I tolerate your passion for curry!
You are understanding about my mum's disability
You helped my dad lay his patio

You will notice that some of these items are very specific (such as liking curry or laying a patio), while others are vaguer (such as talking and feeling able to trust). This kind of list often throws up these two different kinds of things to celebrate. This is because the specific items tend to build up and create the vaguer items. For instance, Clare and Lewis like clubbing, ten pin bowling, sending e-mails and so on. These are the everyday activities that promote the creation of trust, communication and caring. The list also reflects contacts with the wider community – friends and parents, for instance. These shared networks help Clare and Lewis to feel part of something greater than just the two of them, and this sense of connection in turn helps them to feel like an item – a reality rather than something still not quite formed.

Once you have created your list, think about how you can boost the things you already feel good about. For example, Clare and

Lewis could put special time aside to play ten pin bowling each week. They could also invite friends to go clubbing with them in order to build on two items they see as valuable. They could use the knowledge that their dogs like each other to develop new activities like walking or dog training. Lewis could even teach Clare the finer points of curry appreciation! All of this can help the relationship to feel strong and secure. Clare and Lewis could also act on the items about good communication and trust by regularly sharing how important this is to the two of them.

Sometimes it can help to dissect what makes something so good in a relationship. For example, Clare and Lewis might ask themselves why they find it easy to talk to one another. Lewis might say that it is because Clare listens carefully and does not jump in with her own opinion at every moment, but that she is not afraid to challenge something she does not agree with. Clare might say that she values the way in which Lewis takes her point of view seriously and helps her reflect on what she is talking about. It can be useful to undertake this kind of exercise as it can help if the relationship runs into difficulty in the future. Stress or tension – perhaps because of illness or a work problem – can rob a couple of their usual easy manner of talking to one another, and remembering what you have identified as helping mutual communication can get you back on track.

Solve problems

Difficulties of varying degrees are actually extremely common in new relationships. This is counter to the romantic fairytale of a couple who fall in love and live happily ever after! New relationships need a period of emotional settling down and sorting before they run more smoothly (although every couple will encounter difficulties at different stages throughout a relationship). It is not so much the actual problems that a couple may face, but the way in which the problems are handled that influences how a new couple feel about their relationship.

CASE STUDY

Roger and Evelyn met through a specialist dating agency for people who had been divorced. Roger had divorced some years before, but Evelyn was a comparatively new divorcee, having only divorced six months before applying to the agency. At their first meeting they got on very well indeed, finding lots of topics in common, and they soon made arrangements to date regularly. All went swimmingly for four months. Then they tried to talk about what they wanted to do together over the imminent Christmas period. Roger had two daughters whom he wanted to spend most of Christmas visiting. Evelyn had no children, and asked to spend Christmas with Roger and his daughters. Roger told Evelyn that he thought this was a bad idea as it might lead them to think their father had a committed relationship when he himself was not sure that he and Evelyn had reached this stage. Evelyn was very upset. She had hoped that Roger felt as committed as she did, and wanted to begin to get to know his daughters in preparation for being around Roger more in the future. She felt that Roger was hiding her away rather than integrating her into his life. The result was that Evelyn spent a miserable Christmas Day alone, while Roger felt sad that he had upset Evelyn, although he still felt he did not want to involve Evelyn with his daughters until he was ready.

Roger and Evelyn made some classic mistakes about handling their potential difficulties:

- They made assumptions about what each of them felt about the relationship. Roger thought that Evelyn was happy to go out with him, but was not ready for a longer commitment, because that was how he felt. Evelyn thought Roger wanted the higher level of commitment that she wanted. Once these unspoken assumptions were exposed, the problem seemed harder to manage.
- Neither partner explained the problem to the other. Roger stuck to his original decision without helping Evelyn to understand why he felt the way he did, while Evelyn found it hard to say why she had thought Roger was as committed as she was.

- They did not see the problem coming. Certain events through-out the year can raise particular issues for couples, particularly where there may be ex-partners, children or other relatives in-volved. Christmas is definitely one of these times, as are birthdays, anniversaries, public holidays and school holidays.
- They found it hard to share what they were feeling about the situation. Evelyn felt isolated, while Roger felt guilty about what had happened.

Managing a problem

Evelyn and Roger could have managed their difficulties more easily and caused each other less hurt. Here are some of the concerns they might have tackled:

Making assumptions

Making an assumption about what your new partner is thinking or feeling is dangerous. In a long-term relationship it can some-times be justified because you will know your partner more intimately, although even in these circumstances you should always check out any assumptions you have made. But in a new relationship it is always important to ask your partner what is going on in their feelings and thoughts. People sometimes avoid this because they do not want to hear an answer that is counter to their own dreams and hopes – Evelyn may have avoided telling Roger that she wanted a long-term relationship with him because she sensed he was less sure about this. If you want your relation-ship to run smoothly, it is important to be brave and talk about subjects that may seem tricky. Not only will you get a clearer picture of where the relationship is going, but it will be good practice for the future if you need to discuss issues later.

Explain the problem

When two people try to talk about a difficulty they often become tongue-tied, saying things like 'well, you know what I mean' or 'do I have to spell this out?' Sometimes this is born out of a fear of upsetting the partner, and then having to deal with the emotional fallout, or a reluctance to engage in protracted discussions about something potentially embarrassing. But if you can explain the problem in a simple way it can help you and your partner to deal with a difficulty more easily. Roger might have said something like 'I am very fond of you Evelyn, but my children have already been hurt by a broken relationship in the past. I do not want them to grow fond of you, only for us to discover that we do not want to stay together. I feel I need longer to make that judgement. Perhaps we can talk about this in more detail after Christmas?' This kind of straightforward statement is honest and thoughtful. Notice it also suggests that Roger and Evelyn should discuss their commitment to one another at a later date. This gives Evelyn hope that Roger is not about to call things off. Explaining in this way is not likely to immediately change everything, but it provides a starting point for both partners and helps to clarify the situation.

Seeing the problem
The ability to see a problem coming is an art that not all couples develop. Many couples treat their life together as if they are riding a horse without reins or stirrups – they let the horse go where it wants, sometimes throwing them off, because they lack control. I am not suggesting that you turn into a 'control freak' trying to manage every single element of your lives together. This would not only feel constricting to the two of you, but could also be extremely boring. But looking ahead and thinking about how you might manage a particular issue can help to shrink its negative effect on your life. For example, Roger and Evelyn might have talked about handling Christmas at least a month before instead of trying to untangle their assumptions and expectations the week before. This approach buys time to rethink attitudes and sort out solutions long before the problem becomes a major stumbling block.

Sharing the problem
Sharing a problem means allowing yourself to acknowledge the emotion involved in what is happening. If Roger or Evelyn had been able to explain that they felt guilty or sad it could have helped them to make sense of what they were going through and

aided their empathy towards one another. Of itself, showing emotion rarely solves problems. Sometimes it can appear to cloud the issue, but it is a crucial part of any decision-making process that you enter into. Some research suggests that emotions actually drive our decision-making process in the brain, even when emotion does not appear to be present, for example when positioning a car on the road. So to ignore the emotion involved in a problem is to cut out a crucial part of the issues you face.

Frequent problems encountered by new couples

There are a number of difficulties that come up for new couples more frequently than other issues. Here are some that you might encounter, with some instant solutions.

Money

Once you are past the first date, you may find that who pays for what and when becomes a real difficulty. I suggest you stick to sharing the costs of whatever you do until you are very confident that the relationship has a future and that you know your partner well. Never lend money or credit cards to a new partner, or give them access to your bank account, even if you are madly in love (in fact, particularly if you are madly in love, as your judgement is bound to be skewed). Remember, getting to know someone well takes months rather than days or hours. If they are honourable they will understand your desire to keep things on an even footing.

Sex

As you have read in Chapter Six, starting a sexual relationship needs careful handling. If you face problems about sex – perhaps because one partner wants it more quickly than the other – always be guided by the 'slower to decide' partner. This may seem slightly frustrating at first, but it can prevent a toxic dose of regret from invading the relationship and it demonstrates mutual commitment to finding the right time. If you run into other sex problems (see Chapter Six) the best approach is to try and talk about them as soon as possible. This can seem embarrassing, but facing what is happening can be the first step to sorting the issue out. Always remember to practise safe sex and, when appropriate, insist that your partner also does.

Communication

Problems with talking to each other can bubble up after the first love-struck stage that many new couples experience. They may have spent the first weeks existing on 'extra sensory perception', or willing themselves to believe that this is 'the one', and talking can come as something of a novelty. But the fact is that no relationship can survive if the partners do not invest in talking to each other about serious and not so serious matters. You may think it would be nice to understand what your boyfriend or girlfriend is saying by meaningful looks alone, but this will not hold water for long, and soon the relationship will founder. Encourage time to talk by creating space in the day when you are not with others or engaged in an activity that takes your attention. Ensure you are both reasonably relaxed – talking in depth is very hard to do when you are both shattered after a long day at work or engaged in domestic activities. Set the scene by making sure you are comfortable and can maintain eye contact, as well as ensuring that other distractions are removed.

What do you both want now?

Now you have survived the early dating phase, talking about what kind of relationship you both want is not necessarily easy, for a number of reasons:

- You may both wonder how the other is feeling about the relationship.
- You may not want to reveal strong feelings in case they are not returned.
- You may want to ask a specific question about your partner's behaviour (such as 'why haven't I met your parents yet?' or 'why can't I phone you at work?') but worry that this will seem intrusive or insensitive.

- You may have a strong sense that you want something different to your new boyfriend or girlfriend.

Avoiding these relationship traps can be hard, but there are some things you can do to help you feel less embarrassed or anxious about addressing the immediate future:

- Use 'open questions'. For instance, ask 'I wonder how you feel about our relationship now?' rather than 'I suppose you want to end the relationship now?' The former style of question allows the listener to talk about the full range of their feelings as opposed to the second form – a closed question – that can only really be answered with a yes or no, closing down conversation.
- Ask your partner to make a list of the things they would like to ask you about now that you know each other better. You can also undertake this exercise. Take turns to read out a topic from the lists, and then discuss whatever comes up. Try to be honest and straightforward.
- Ask your partner about past relationships. Avoid interrogating them about how many boyfriends or girlfriends they have had, but ask them if the relationships lasted, how they felt about the various people they may have been out with and what they felt helped any of their previous relationships to succeed.
- Share what you feel is going well in your relationship, and where you would like to make some changes. It is important to celebrate and reinforce the good things about your relationship by talking about and remembering them. There is some evidence to suggest that couples who are able to remember their early days with fond memories, and talk together about the importance of that stage in their lives, are more likely to stay together.

Spotting relationships that are working and those that may be in trouble

This probably sounds a rather obvious topic. You could be forgiven for saying 'I think I can spot whether my relationships are OK or not.' But in my experience of counselling, people often do miss some of the signs that distinguish between a relationship that is going well and one that is heading into stormy waters. This is sometimes because of external circumstances. For instance, your parents or children may like your partner so much, and you may want to please them, that you miss obvious signs that the relationship is not going as smoothly as it should. Or you may be caught up with extra pressure at work that causes you to put your relationship on the back-burner. Whatever the reason, if you can spot the signs quickly you are more likely to be able to correct the problem and to decide if you want to carry on. If you can also tell when the relationship is going well, you can concentrate on those aspects that make you both especially happy.

When your relationship is:

Looking good	Not so good
You feel able to talk to each other about most topics with ease.	You find it hard to communicate, and know that some topics are taboo.
You feel able to trust your partner not to let you down, and have specific examples of this over a period of more than three months.	You are not sure if you can trust your partner, and can think of a number of specific occasions when they have let you down badly.
You feel you know something about their background, and have had this authenticated by meeting his or her family or friends.	You know little about their background, or have some information, but have not had this authenticated. He or she makes excuses to prevent you meeting family or friends.
Your partner has never asked you to give or lend them money (except amounts of less than £10).	Your partner has asked you to give or lend him or her money, and makes excuses about paying you back.
He or she is respectful towards you and is caring about your needs, beliefs or culture.	He or she often makes fun of you, and seems uncaring about your needs, beliefs or background.
He or she is not bullying or demanding.	He or she has shown signs of bullying or verbal aggression or has made demands they know are distressing to you.

Looking good	Not so good
If you have a sexual relationship, he or she is thoughtful, cares about your sexual satisfaction and is respectful of sexual practices that you are not comfortable with.	If you have a sexual relationship, he or she seems disinterested in pleasing you and asks for sexual practices you are not comfortable with. They may also have pressured you into a sexual relationship.
He or she is understanding about the other demands in your life, such as children, other relatives, work and other commitments.	He or she seems uncaring about the other commitments in your life, and often demands to come first even when this is extremely difficult.
He or she has shown little sign of jealousy and can cope with you seeing your own friends without them around.	He or she wants you to cut off relationships with friends, or one particular friend, and often monopolises your time.

If you can count more than six in the 'Looking good' column this indicates that you are doing well, and should continue to develop the relationship. If you have more than six in the 'Not so good' column, there is something seriously amiss that needs urgent attention. If you have found just one or two items you know are either missing or causing you anxiety, now is the time to devote some energy to sorting these out. If your partner does not co-operate with you, this gives you a powerful message about their potential commitment to the relationship.

Perhaps the most important element in creating a successful relationship is to have a good sense of your own self-worth. Without self-worth you might settle for a relationship that you know in your heart is not right for you, believe that you should put up with some of the behaviours in the 'Not so good' column above or find it hard to ask for what you want from a relationship. Gaining a sense of self-worth or self-esteem is rightly the subject of a whole book of its own, but good self-esteem breaks down into four main areas for you to work on: physical, social, emotional and mental (see Chapter Two).

In addition, everybody has a spiritual aspect to their personality. By this I do not mean that everybody has a set of religious beliefs

– clearly they do not – but everyone has a set of beliefs, morals and ethics that allows them to manage life. Sometimes these beliefs are supportive and help them to make wise decisions about how to handle the big (and often smaller) events of life – death, birth, commitment and so on. If you feel secure in your spiritual vision, your sense of self-worth will be high. If you find it hard to use the beliefs you have inherited or created, you may feel at odds with the world. By this I am not suggesting you should not question beliefs or ideas in the world around you. Asking questions and struggling to make sense of what 'it' all means can be a source of enrichment in exactly the same way that some people find blind acceptance helpful. But if you feel spiritually impoverished, take some time to think about why you live your life the way you do and whether there are certain parts that need working on. It can help to learn about the ways in which other people have managed this over the millennia, so consider looking for material that will inform you as you search for spiritual renewal.

Read more about these concerns, and how they influence your choice of partner, in Chapter Two.

Attachments and their problems

In your search for a loving partner you may find yourself attracted to a partner who is already attached to someone else. This is part of human nature. We cannot switch off attraction. Something about the way a person looks, their character and personality or their lifestyle, can make them seem very attractive. But if that person is already attached to another – married to, living with or going out with someone – our attraction can become a problem rather than a pleasure.

CASE STUDY
Lorna met Danny through her work as a physiotherapist. Danny came to the hospital where she worked to undertake some repairs, and Lorna was instantly attracted. Danny was cheeky and flirty with her, and they arranged to meet at a local pub for a drink one lunch break. Danny came on to Lorna in a big way, telling her

how gorgeous she was and how pleased he was to have met her. She and Danny began to meet regularly, often spending evenings at pubs and clubs all over the city they lived in. And then the bombshell dropped. Lorna was out shopping one Saturday morning when she spotted Danny. He was with a woman and pushing a buggy with a toddler in it. Something made Lorna avoid meeting him, but when he called round later in the week, she demanded to know who the woman was. Lorna had hoped against hope that it was a sister or friend, but Danny admitted it was his wife and son. Lorna was shell-shocked. She was even more taken aback when Danny said that his marriage need make no difference – they could go on seeing each other in the same way as before. Lorna knew she was tempted – she really fancied Danny – but could not square this with her own code of behaviour and so she told him it was over. A friend later confided that Danny was well known for his affairs, and that she was well out of the relationship.

Relationships with attached people are usually fraught with problems. You will probably run the emotional gauntlet of guilt, anxiety, euphoria and jealousy. You may find yourself doing a lot of waiting around for a lover who is only partially available to you. None of this makes a relationship easy to manage. The best advice I can give you is to be honest with yourself about the mutual attraction, but consider whether you must act on it. If you put the positives and negatives about such relationships in the scales, I am afraid the negatives will weigh heavier, especially if your prospective partner has children. If, despite this, you still want a relationship, tell your partner you will only consider this if they are not in their current relationship. If they cannot make the commitment to be with you in this way, then the relationship is probably never going to get off the ground. I suggest you avoid them and find a relationship where you can be top of the list, instead of somewhere near the bottom.

This also applies to the relationship (if it can be called that) that you may make at the office party or some other social gathering where drink is running freely. If you do share a drunken snog with someone, this should be apologised for in the clear light of day and then forgotten. For a relationship to really have a good start, you both need to be in your right mind, not 'under the influence'! If you are both free, and want to take things further, arrange a date as if this was the first time you had met, rather than making the assumption that you now know each other intimately because of a grope in the stationery cupboard.

In conclusion

This chapter has looked at the future of your new relationship, focussing on the four stages of new relationships, strategies for survival during these four stages and understanding what happens now you have established a new relationship. You have also looked at building strengths and working on problems, spotting relationship signs that indicate whether the relationship is working well or needs attention and the importance of self-esteem in relationships. Finally, you have considered relationships with people who are already attached to others.

8

Have You Got a Problem? Your Most Common Questions Answered

This last chapter is aimed at answering some of the most common problems that people encounter in finding new partners and then managing the early stages of their relationship. The questions and answers are grouped in sections that correspond to the chapters of this book. This is to enable you to look for more detailed advice and support in the appropriate chapter. Each question and answer examines a specific difficulty. Although this may not be identical to your concern, it could help your understanding to read and identify with some of the issues described in the question.

Finding and sustaining new relationships

Marie, 30
Q
I come from a family with a history of broken relationships. My parents divorced, as have both my older sisters. Does this mean that I am likely to find myself in the same position once I find a partner and establish a relationship?

A

Not at all. It is true that the influence of your parents' experience on how you form relationships can be strong, but you have taken an important first step by thinking about how you might have been affected. When you begin a new relationship, you might find it helpful to consider whether the difficulties faced by your family have a theme. For example, did they have problems in communicating? Showing affection? Discussing money? If you can identify some of these, you could watch for any warning sign that you are experiencing problems in this area. It is also important to think about practical steps you might take to learn how to manage these problem areas before you meet them in a relationship.

John, 42

Q

I have always believed that my partner should rely on me to do the traditional things that men do on dates – open doors, pay for the meal or tickets and then see them safely home. This is partly because my father was just this kind of man. But my last date told me I was patronising and old-fashioned. I have had a string of relationships that never really lasted more than one or two meetings. Am I really as I was described, and could this be the reason for the failure of my dates?

A

It may not be the main reason for the failure of your dates, but it could be that women of today perceive your courtesy as a slur on their abilities. They may feel that your insistence on looking after them implies that they are not capable or independent enough to look after themselves. I suggest you try to continue caring for the women you meet, but show this by listening attentively to what they want talk to you about, telling them about your own interests and lifestyle and then asking their opinion about the film, play or meal you have just shared. I am sure that there is a woman somewhere who is looking for a polite and caring man like yourself, so keep trying!

Tina, 26

Q

I am in a comparatively new relationship of four months' duration. My partner and I get on really well, except for one thing. We argue about money. I feel that I pay a disproportionate amount of money towards our dates. Recently we went away for a weekend in a country hotel, and I ended up paying for the whole enterprise. I don't want him to pay for everything, but I do want him to share the costs of going out together.

A

New relationships can often throw up this kind of problem. Often they occur because of unspoken assumptions about what the relationship is, and what it holds for the future. The first thing you need to do is to try the simple approach. Say clearly that you want to split the costs of dates straight down the middle. Do this without shouting or demanding. Keep calm, and your message will be much clearer. The next thing to do is to ask yourself what the money issue is actually telling you about the relationship. For instance, do you feel you are putting much more emotionally into the relationship than your new partner? Are you unsure about the footing that you began the relationship on? If these issues do seem important, make some time to talk about your concerns with your partner. This may not be easy, but it could help to straighten out any problems you have before they become entrenched.

Luke, 33

Q

I find it very hard to meet new people and often feel lonely and resentful about my lack of social life. I regularly visit my local pub and belong to a walking club, but I know everyone in these groups already. How can I meet new people, and perhaps a new partner?

A

You need to spread your net more widely than you do at present. If you only do the same things week after week it stands to reason that you will not meet new people. One way to approach this is to think of an interest you may have (apart from walking) and look for a class or club that would allow you to explore this. Ask at your local Further Education College for information. You could also consider using your current interests to meet new people. For instance, take a walking holiday (several tour companies run these abroad) or visit different pubs in your locality. Pick a quiz night or a karaoke evening as people will be expecting visitors on these evenings and will welcome you with greater warmth. If you take this advice, remember to take the initiative and reach out to those around you, as this can be a step towards creating friendships.

Alice, 19

Q

I am a student at university and feel like I am the only person without a boyfriend. From a personal point of view, I am not too worried about this. I am enjoying the social life and my studies are on track. But everybody in my hall of residence seems to have a boyfriend, and I do sometimes feel left out. Do you think I should find someone to go out with so I can be like the others?

A

Forcing yourself to find a partner in order to fit in is a waste of your time and resources. As you say yourself, you are enjoying the social and study sides of university life, so you have nothing to worry about. If you feel that you have a narrow circle of friends (perhaps only those in your hall of residence) I suggest you look to take part in other groups around the university – perhaps through sport or drama, for instance. This will give you access to a larger circle of friends, and take some of the pressure of wanting to fit in with a small group off your shoulders. You will find a partner when the time is right for you.

For more information on these topics turn to Chapter One.

What kind of relationship do you want?

Lucy, 34

Q

I have always seen myself as a placid person, and had partners who were fairly quiet. But I have just started dating a wonderful man who is completely different. He is outgoing and has a great social life that I am pleased to be part of. The problem is that he has mood swings – one moment up, the next down. I am not sure how to handle this as I do not have a lot of experience of being with someone like this. Any suggestions?

A

Many people who are very socially active seem to experience ups and downs in mood. This may be because they are boosting the side of themselves that wants a good time, causing a slump when the 'show' is over. It may be that he is attracted to you precisely because of your placid and level nature, maybe even hoping that some of this will rub off on him. I suggest you talk to him about the mood changes. Try not to be accusative, or suggest he has to change, but ask him how he feels about this behaviour, and what he would like you to do in response. He may want you to simply be around, or to listen to him if he wants to talk about how he is feeling. You could also suggest that he has periods of less intense partying, when he relaxes with you. Plan simple activities to do together – a quiet meal at a favourite restaurant, a picnic in the country, or an evening at home snuggled up with a bottle of wine. These could all help him to feel less up and down and more on an even keel. This will also help you to feel more secure in the relationship.

Eric, 31

Q

I have been cohabiting with Rachel for five years and want her to marry me. She has so far refused, saying she is happy with things as they are. I think this suggests a lack of commitment, and I am now worried she will leave me. Should I tell her to marry me or leave?

A

I don't think you can tell someone to marry you. She obviously feels happy with the situation as it is, and clearly feels committed to you and the relationship or she would not have stuck around for five years. It might be helpful to discover why she does not feel ready to marry. It is possible that she wants never to marry, but nevertheless wants a committed long-term relationship with you or that she might feel ready to marry later. But forcing her to make a decision or demanding that she agrees to marry you will destroy the affection you have for one another, so be patient as you try to understand more about her feelings.

Harriet, 50

Q

I feel I lack confidence in the dating process since my last boyfriend split up with me. I was married for twelve years, and since my divorce two years ago, have had a number of boyfriends. None of them seem to last very long, and I have begun to think there is something wrong with me. What can I do?

A

Getting over a divorce can take a long time, often much longer than people imagine. I suspect you are still feeling sore after the break-up and may not be ready to make a new relationship. I am not suggesting you should not see men for dates, but that you need to have a different mental attitude towards them. It is possible that your boyfriends have understood, perhaps subconsciously, that you are looking for some sense of security. This may have been a bit too much for them, and so they have backed off. I think you may need more time to work through your divorce, and perhaps to slow down on the dating scene while you do this. You may find it helpful to see a counsellor in order to help you sort out your feelings about the past.

George, 36

Q

I think I attract the wrong type of man. I am an outgoing and bubbly kind of person, but really want a secure and long-lasting relationship. Unfortunately, I seem to attract men who just want a 'good time', by which they generally mean sex. What am I doing wrong?

A

I don't think you are doing anything wrong. After all you are just being yourself. If you are an extrovert, this is often very attractive to others, but this is no reason for you to alter your character, even if you could do this. The men themselves are responsible for their attitudes, not you. I wonder if you are spending a lot of time mixing with the same people? If you are, try going out with different friends, or look for places where you could meet people with a different attitude. You might also suit an introduction agency, where you could state that you are looking for a secure relationship, and hopefully be matched to a man who also wants this.

You can find more information on these topics in Chapter Two.

What have I learnt from past relationships?

Gail, 25

Q

I have been in a long-term relationship for almost two years with a man, Paul, who was previously divorced. We have a fairly good relationship except that he often becomes withdrawn and quiet if I disagree with him about anything. I have asked him why this happens, but the most information he gives me is to say that his ex-wife was very argumentative. Can you help me make sense of his behaviour?

A

Paul has a learned response to conflict and disagreement. He seems to have learnt that the only way to cope with this kind of problem is to put down the emotional shutters and wait for the storm to blow over. I suspect that he has been hurt by his ex-wife's behaviour, and could not stop the arguing by using any other method. You will need to be extremely patient, and help him to understand that the occasional disagreement is to be expected in most relationships. You can help him by listening respectfully to his point of view on any issue, never shouting or bullying in order to force him back to your point of view and asking his opinion when possible. Gradually he may gain in confidence as you give him the respect he seems to have lacked in his marriage.

Gita, 31

Q

My family are very caring and loving, but I am married to a man who hardly ever shows his feelings. I know he loves me, but he seems to find it hard to tell me how he feels, even in the privacy of our bedroom. I find this hurtful, but he says I should know how he feels and stop asking him to confirm it. Is he right?

A

To some extent, you are both right. He has obviously come from a family who do not show their feelings very much. If he is from an Asian-Indian background, this is perfectly normal and accept-able family tradition. In fact, in some traditions, to show feeling publicly to a wife is a mark of disrespect to the wife. But you come from a different background and he needs to understand that you have different expectations. I suggest you consider a compromise. Explain that you understand his feelings, but that you need some sign of his affection or you feel cut off from him. Tell him what you need – a hug or kiss, perhaps a kind word – and say that this can be a private matter between the two of you. He may find it easier if you are specific about your needs rather than vague, as this vagueness may cause him to feel that you have huge needs he cannot meet.

Lucas, 20

Q

When I was fourteen I had a real crush on a girl at school. She was in the year above me, and I thought she was gorgeous. We never went out together, and I have lost touch with my school-friends since moving house, but my feelings for her seem to get in the way of any relationship I have nowadays. No other girl seems to measure up. Will I get over these feelings?

A

The problem with your feelings are that they are based on an idealisation. You never really got to know this girl, and so she has become a fantasy in your mind, probably growing in stature as you have got older. It is no wonder that no other girl can measure up because they are being compared to a saint! You have two choices – either to spend a lot of time tracing the girl you liked, probably to find she is with someone else anyway, or to try to enjoy the women you do meet, and take pleasure in their attributes for what they are, instead of comparing them with a dream. Next time you meet someone new, make a mental list of all the good things about them rather than all their shortcomings. It is also possible that you are unconsciously using your memories as a protection against rejection or disappointment. Happily, life is always a risk – that's part of its fun as well as its challenge. Allow yourself to take some risks and you may feel much more able to make satisfying relationships.

Patrick, 28

Q

I find my new partners' attitude to her parents intensely annoying. I visit my parents regularly and phone them frequently. She hardly ever makes contact, and although I have taken her to visit mine a few times, she refuses to take me to meet her parents. Could this difference mean we are not suited to each other?

A

Your differences over attitudes to parents may not mean that the relationship is in trouble, but they could be telling you something important about the stage of relationship you are in. I suspect that you are trying to push the relationship into a more committed phase, and that this is too fast for your partner. Taking a partner to visit parents is, after all, traditionally an event that only takes place when the relationship is reasonably established. It is also possible that you want to exert some control over your partner. This may be because you have been hurt in the past by a partner who took little account of what was important to you, or because you fear the loss of your new partner. Whatever the reason, you need to relax and let your partner have her own way of relating to her parents, just as she needs to be tolerant of yours. Eventually you will find that you develop more understanding about your shared values and ideals, but these need time to come to fruition.

Learn more about these topics by reading Chapter Three.

Who is right for me? And how do I find them?

Susan, 41

Q

I feel as if I am drawn to relationships with men who do not seem to want to go out with me. I often spend weeks fancying a man I have met, only to find that he is hardly aware I exist. I have been engaged twice, but both relationships petered out. I am often asked out, but tend not to fancy these men! I travel all over the world with my company, meeting lots of new people every year, so why can't I find a man who returns my interest?

A

I think you are a romantic! You are dreaming of an ideal – a prince on a white horse – who will sweep you off your feet. The men you do meet, ordinary but pleasant, have no hope of living up to this vision, and this is why the relationship folds up. It is also likely that your fast-moving job is contributing to your confusion. You meet so many people it must be akin to being a child in a sweet shop – the choice must sometimes be bewildering. Perhaps your dreams about the men you fancy are an escape from the pressure of meeting so many people at such a rate. Next time you are asked out, unless you are actually repelled, accept the date and look for the qualities your date possesses. Alternatively, be more assertive in asking out the men you fancy, rather than waiting for them to notice you. In this way you should allow yourself to experience the reality of your dreams, and this can help you to make choices about future relationships. Try not to look too far into the future. Enjoy the relationships for what they are rather than building them into sky-high expectations that can only be dashed by real life.

William, 33

Q

I am going out with a woman aged fifty. We get on extremely well and really enjoy each other's company. The problem is that my friends think I am mad. They are always trying to persuade me to link up with a woman of my own age, but I am happy as I am. Should I take their advice or ignore their prejudice?

A

I think you know the answer to this. If you are both happy, and the age gap does not cause either of you significant problems, then I think you should carry on together. Your friends are prejudiced, chiefly because they fear difference or someone who dares to step outside the norm set by their group. Try introducing your girlfriend to your friends in a neutral setting – perhaps at a shared meal. Let them see how much she means to you and some of the teasing and prejudice should die down.

Rhona, 27

Q

My friend has a common relationship pattern that I am worried I am emulating. She meets men, uses them to have a good time – clubbing, parties, holidays and so on – and then breaks up with them. My past two relationships have followed a very similar pattern. Could this happen to me? I don't want to have this kind of relationship pattern.

A
The fact that you have recognised that you do not want the same style of relationship is a positive sign. It is easy in a group, or with a particular friend, to find that you are doing the same kind of things in order to fit in or to identify with an individual. While I would not want to suggest you should never see this friend again, perhaps some time spent with other friends would not come amiss. It can also help to look for couples known to you who have a style of relationship that you would like for yourself. Notice what makes them good role models – can they talk easily to one another? Do they share a sense of humour? Can they argue without sulking for hours? Then, when you begin a new relationship, try to incorporate this behaviour with your new partner. Reinforcing the attributes you want in a relationship, and minimising the ones you don't, can help you to break out of a negative pattern and give you the relationship you want.

Angela, 24
Q
When I begin going out with someone I am often very quiet. I am not sure why this happens as I am not a particularly quiet person in other circumstances. Past boyfriends have commented on this, and told me that they had to get to know a very different person to the one they first met, and that this was disconcerting. Why do you think I do this?

A
It is difficult to make an absolute judgement about why this happens, but you may simply be biding your time, waiting to see what your new partner is like. This is rather like holding all your emotional cards close to your chest, buying yourself time before you have to declare your real self. This may have some psychological benefits for you – you can avoid having your real self

trampled over if you have made a poor choice, or can end a relationship with most of your self-esteem still intact. However, it could also mean that you are putting men off because they sense they are not getting your 'genuine' self, and they give up on the relationship. You may be afraid of being hurt, but I think this fear can be balanced with the pleasure of enjoying being yourself in a relationship. Let yourself go a bit, and you may be surprised at the results!

Read more on these topics in Chapter Four.

The dating game

Myra, 30
Q
My friend Becky is always trying to drag me along to blind dates. She seems to have a secret store of men whom she drags out to meet me. Most of them are just not my cup of tea, but I can't tell her this as it would really hurt her. How can I avoid these ghastly dates?

A
You are going to have to be brave and tell Becky that you do not want to take part in any more blind dates. She probably feels that she is helping you, so unless you are honest the dates will go on arriving! Say something like 'I am grateful for your kindness in arranging blind dates, but I have decided not to do this any more. I would prefer to find my own dates, but perhaps we can go out in a foursome one day?' In this way you can maintain your friendship, but avoid the dates you dislike.

David, 27
Q
I have been friends with Janet for about five years. We were at college together, studying for work-related exams, and then we met again at a college social do. We go for a drink together most weeks, and talk about our work and social life. We have both had relationships during this time, but neither of us are in one at the

moment. I feel as if I am falling in love with Janet. This feeling has been creeping up on me for the last few months, but I have no idea if Janet feels the same way. If I tell her, could it be the end of a great friendship? It will kill me if we break up because I have misread the situation.

A

I suspect it might hurt you very much if you do not reveal your feelings. You could spend the rest of your life wondering 'What if . . . ?' when you could have the relationship you really want. Pick a time when you can talk to Janet without interruption and explain how you feel. She may be surprised, but don't worry if she seems a bit taken aback. Ask her how she feels, or arrange to meet up again when she has had time to think things through. The alternative to this approach is to write her a letter, but this is less effective because it creates a physical and emotional distance between you that you will ultimately have to overcome.

Elaine, 55

Q

I have been corresponding with a man I made contact with through a lonely hearts magazine and he now wants us to meet. I am not sure how I feel about this. He sounds very pleasant and thoughtful, and even sent me a bouquet for my birthday, but it is a long time since I met a man for a date. Both of us are widowed, having lost our partners about five years ago. I am sure that this shared experience has created a bond between us, but is this enough to warrant meeting up?

A

Providing you follow safe dating practice (see pp. 108–9) I can see no reason why you should not meet up to find out if you want to take things further. Many happy relationships begin with an exchange of letters (or e-mail nowadays). Just be aware that you may feel as if you know each other well, but getting to know each other face to face will be a different matter. Take your time and you will find your confidence will grow. Don't jump to conclusions about what you want to happen, be honest with yourself about what you want from the relationship and you should enjoy meeting your correspondent.

Paul, 32

Q

A woman at my office keeps asking me out. She has even sent me sexy e-mails and notes. I do not want to go out with her, but she will not take no for an answer. What can I do?

A

If she is this persistent, you may actually have a sexual harassment case brewing. I suggest you talk to your Personnel Department in confidence about your problems. Explain that you do not want to get her into trouble, but do want to stop the dating invites. They can then deal with the situation on your behalf.

Rita, 26

Q

I recently went on a wonderful date with a man I really liked. Now he has asked me to go out with him again, and I find myself stalling. I am puzzled by my reaction. I would like to see him again, but find myself putting off making a firm arrangement to meet. Can you explain why I feel this way?

A

It is strange, but sometimes a wonderful first date sets a precedent that individuals may fear can never be met again. You may be delaying because you fear that it was 'all too good to be true' and wonder if it could all go wrong next time. This may be because you have a slightly pessimistic nature or because you have experienced this in the past. I suggest you arrange a second date, and allow yourself to believe that you have met someone you could be really happy with. Focus on the things you really like or enjoy together, and remember that you are only just at the start of getting to know this new man in your life.

Read more on these topics in Chapter Five.

Getting closer – dating and intimacy

Natalie, 17

Q

I have been going out with a boy of eighteen for a year and although we have been intimate sexually, we have never had intercourse. Lately he has dropped a lot of hints about 'doing it' and suggested that I should want this too. I am not sure how I feel about it, but am worried he could leave me if I do not agree. Should I have sex with him?

A

If you are not sure then you should not have sex with him. It is not clear why he has started suggesting that you take this next step, but it could be pressure from friends or a feeling that he is 'mature' enough to do this. This is all very well, but if you are not at the same stage, then your first lovemaking could be a disaster rather than a pleasure. Explain that you are not ready, but this does not mean you feel less interested in him. If he cares for you, he will understand that you need to feel more sure about having sex with him. When you do feel ready, make sure you practise safe sex (see pp. 131–2 for guidelines on this).

Wendy, 36

Q

I enjoy making love with my partner but am worried that he is not enjoying it as much as me. We are comparatively new lovers (we only started making love four weeks ago after being together three months) and he seems very quiet. Most of our lovemaking is done in silence. Should I expect him to talk more? And how can I encourage him to be more responsive?

A

How people behave in bed is just as much a part of their person-ality as how they behave elsewhere. It may be that he is not a very talkative person, but is enjoying the sex as much as you. Or it could be that he is still slightly uncertain about how to respond sexually. It often takes some time for new lovers to get used to each other. When you make love, try asking him if he likes what you are doing, or tell him how much you are enjoying his seduction. Avoid demanding 'sexual information', as this will simply put him off talking to you at all. Instead, ask in a gentle way as you caress him. If you feel confident about the relationship, you might also try asking him, when you are not in bed together, about his feelings regarding sex. This will take some tact and diplomacy, but a frank conversation of this type can help to open up the subject, providing you approach the issue carefully. As your relationship matures, you will probably find that you become better able to interpret each other's feelings and desires, so a little encouragement to talk now could pay dividends later.

Nyree, 52

Q

My partner and I have been together for about six months. We have a fairly good sex life, but it is marred by a problem I am experiencing. Every time he enters me during intercourse it feels painful. The pain is like a pinch, or sometimes a dragging sensation. What could be causing this? It is really spoiling an otherwise OK sex life.

A

It is a strong possibility that you are experiencing this pain because of the menopause. At your age, the supply of oestrogen in the body declines, and this can cause the vagina to become dryer. As a first step you could try a lubricant – KY Jelly or Senselle are both excellent and available from reputable chemists. If this does not help, ask your GP for further assistance. He or she may be able to prescribe an oestrogen cream for use in the vagina or suggest hormone replacement therapy (HRT) which can prevent this kind of dryness. You should combine these approaches with lovemaking that gives you plenty of stimulation, ensuring that you are really aroused before proceeding to intercourse.

Anita, 30

Q

I have been going out with a man, Dave, for the last nine months. I want to start a sexual relationship with him, but he seems very reluctant. We are both unattached and have no children, and he could easily stay overnight at my flat. But he refuses to stay, often leaving in the early hours of the morning after a night out. What am I doing wrong?

A

I do not know if you have asked him why he doesn't want to make love, but I am sure he has a good reason. Perhaps he was hurt in a previous relationship and wants to be sure that he is ready for a commitment to you, or is nervous about lovemaking for some reason. Invite him for a cosy evening in your home and ask him if he can explain why he seems less than keen to sleep with you. If he finds this difficult, be patient, giving him lots of space and time to tell you in his own way. If, after this, he is still not ready for sex, don't push him because this will cause him to back off further. Just let him know you are there for him and will be ready to let him stay the night when he is comfortable with this.

Read more on these topics in Chapter Six.

The future of your new relationship

Marcie, 36

Q

When I first met my new lover I thought he was the greatest thing since sliced bread. Now, six months on, he is really annoying me. At the beginning of our relationship, I saw his outgoing nature as lovely – a really friendly man. Now I just see a man who cannot stop talking and who flirts with every woman he meets. What has happened to the man I thought I knew?

A

Nothing has happened to him! In fact, he is exactly the same man you met, but you have entered the stage of a relationship where you see the other side of what you first thought of as wonderful attributes. Now you have to decide if this is what you want, and can tolerate, because of the good things that balance the relationship, or if you cannot take the relationship further because of the insight you have developed. Because you have seen this side of your lover, you may find that you come to accept his foibles, and that this knowledge actually helps the relationship to move on. I wouldn't give up on the partnership straight away. Stay with it a bit longer and you could find that this stage moves into the next stage where you are better able to take a more holistic view. Don't forget that he may be in exactly the same position as you, wondering where the woman he first met has gone!

Simon, 24

Q

I have been going out with Naomi for eight months, and it is just not working out. I have tried very hard to make the relationship work for me, but I have decided to end it. I know Naomi is going to be very hurt. Would it be better to write and tell her (she lives some distance away) or just ignore her phone calls? I am afraid of her response if I tell her face to face.

A

You are going to have to be brave and bite the bullet, I'm afraid. Writing or ignoring phone calls is only evading the inevitable. It is much better to be honest and tell Naomi that you want to end the relationship. Ask her to visit you and explain that you don't think the relationship can work. Remember to be sensitive and understanding as the news is bound to upset Naomi. Avoid promising to keep in touch or to stay friends. If you know it is over, it is kinder in the long run to say this than make promises you know you cannot keep.

Judith, 40

Q

I have recently met a man I feel strongly attracted to, and know that he feels the same towards me by the way he behaves around me. We have got as far as talking about going on a date, but he is married with three small children. I know it would be wrong to go out with him, but we really get on well and I can't help thinking what a great couple we would make. Should I pursue this relationship?

A

I think you know the answer has to be no. You may feel strongly attracted to each other, but this is no reason to put his marriage in jeopardy. Your relationship would not take place in an emotional vacuum – his wife and children would have to endure great sadness and pain if you pursue a relationship that will inevitably affect them, even if you think you can keep it secret from them. I suggest you tell him you cannot start a relationship with him, and look for a relationship with someone who is available to you in a way that this man is not.

Chris, 19

Q

I have two girlfriends – one at university and one in my home town. I have tried to make a choice between them, but cannot decide which one to give up. I think I love them both, in different ways. Do you think I should try to choose? Or is it OK to go on seeing both of them?

A

Whether you go on seeing both girls depends somewhat on their understanding of their relationship to you. If they expect to be your only girlfriend, then you are betraying both of them. If they accept a more 'open relationship', perhaps seeing other people themselves, then your position is less of a problem. It may be fairer to explain to both of them that you do see other people, or that you want to. This is risky, because they are likely to feel slighted and end the relationship, but it would be fairer. Alternatively, ask for a break from both of the relationships and try to assess which girl you miss most and why. This could help you to make a choice, although you could miss both for different reasons! Honesty is probably the best policy, but you won't avoid some pain along the way if you do tell them. I am afraid you will just have to weather this in order to sort things out.

Antonia, 21

Q

I have been going out for about four months with a boy I met at the local pub. My problem is that my parents disapprove of him because they feel he is not 'good enough for me'. He is out of work at present, and I have a good job at a local solicitors, but we have fun together and I don't think it is my parents' business who I go out with. What do you think? I still live at home.

A

Your parents probably feel they have a right to a say over your partners because you are still living with them. To some extent, they are bound to feel involved in your life because it is lived out on their territory, but all parents tend to care about who their child chooses to be with simply because they are parents. It could help if your parents met the man you are seeing in order to help them feel they can trust him. This is not because you need their approval, but simply a way of calming down the response to a largely unknown quantity. It is also important that you examine your own reasons for going out with someone whom you know your parents will disapprove of. Could it be a small act of rebellion? Do you feel they have too much say in other aspects of your life? If any of this rings a bell it could be the case that you are trying to assert your own character in a situation where you feel over-protected. It could be worth talking to (but not arguing with) your parents about your feelings in order to find a way for all of you to live together in peace.

You can read more about these topics in Chapter Seven.

Afterword

Now that you have read this book you will have tackled many of the issues surrounding finding a partner and establishing a new relationship. I also hope that you will have discovered something about yourself, and what you really want from a relationship, whether that is a long-term commitment or a relationship you know may not last forever.

As a couple counsellor I have met many hundreds of couples. One of the questions I always ask at the start of counselling is 'What attracted you to each other?' It is amazing how many couples find this question extremely difficult to answer. Sometimes the difficulties they are facing have wiped out these pleasant memories, but more often there seems to be a block about acknowledging what it was they discovered about each other when they first met! This book has been all about this time in a new relationship. It is a precious time in the life of any couple, and should be treated with the same attention that most couples give to deciding which house to buy or car to choose. Research also seems to suggest that couples who look back on this period of their life fondly are better able to sustain committed relationships.

It may seem strange to imagine that you can plan and discuss your decision to go on a date or enter into a new relationship in the way described in this book, but thinking in this way need not destroy spontaneity or passion. In fact, because you will feel free of the worries that many new couples struggle with unnecessarily, it can actually create space for you to have the relationship you have always dreamed of. And this is what I hope for you – that the love of your life will be enhanced by having read the advice in this book.

Index